THE JULIAN MESSNER

UNITED STATES

QUESTION AND ANSWER BOOK

THE JULIAN MESSNER

UNITED STATES

QUESTION AND ANSWER BOOK

By Larry Lorimer

Julian Messner  New York

Copyright © 1984 by Larry Lorimer

All rights reserved including the right of
reproduction in whole or in part in any form.
Published by Julian Messner, a Division of Simon & Schuster, Inc.
Simon & Schuster Building,
1230 Avenue of the Americas,
New York, New York 10020.
JULIAN MESSNER and colophon are trademarks of
Simon & Schuster, Inc.

Manufactured in the United States of America

Design by Stanley S. Drate/Folio Graphics Co. Inc.

10   9   8   7   6   5   4   3   2   1

Library of Congress Cataloging in Publication Data.

Lorimer, Lawrence T.
   The Julian Messner United States question and
answer book.

   Includes index.
   Summary: Includes questions and answers about United
States geography, climate, history, places of interest,
people, culture, and other topics.
   1. United States—Miscellanea—Juvenile literature.
[1. United States—Miscellanea.   2. Questions and
answers]   I. Title.   II. Title: United States question
and answer book.
E178.3.L86   1984   973'.076   84-11862

Also available in Wanderer Edition

ISBN: 0-671-53038-0 (Lib. Ed.)
        0-671-52588-3

CONTENTS

1
Beginnings

What is the United States?

The United States of America is one of about 170 countries in the world. It covers a large part of North America. It got its name because it is made up of states that agreed to unite to form one country.

Where is it located?

Most of the United States—forty-eight of the fifty states—forms a large band across the middle section of North America. Alaska, one of the other states, is a large peninsula in the far northwestern corner of North America. Hawaii, the fiftieth state, is a group of islands in the Pacific Ocean some 2,200 miles southwest of the U.S. mainland.

How big is the United States?

The United States covers more than 3½ million square miles. If it were a perfect square, each side of the square would be 1,550 miles long. There is enough land in the United States to form a belt of land nearly 150 miles wide all the way around the earth. If you could stretch the land out into space, you could make a walkway 15 miles wide all the way to the moon.

Does the United States have more land than any other country?

No. The United States is the fourth largest nation, after the Soviet Union, Canada, and China. Two other countries, Brazil and Australia, are only a little smaller than the United States. The six largest countries in area are shown in the following table.

LARGEST COUNTRIES IN THE WORLD

Country	Area in Square Miles
1. Soviet Union	8,649,538
2. Canada	3,849,670
3. China	3,691,514
4. United States	3,615,122
5. Brazil	3,286,488
6. Australia	2,967,909

Most other countries are much smaller than these giants. In fact, there are two independent countries that cover less than *one* square mile. They are the Vatican and Monaco.

How many people live in the United States?

In 1980, when the last full census of the United States was taken, the country had a population of 226,545,000—nearly a quarter of a billion. The estimate of population for 1983 is 231,000,000. If you need to know the present population of a country, state, or city, you should check an up-to-date source, since populations increase rapidly.

Does the United States have more people than any other country?

No. The United States ranks fourth in population. China has by far the largest population in the world with more than one billion people. Next comes India with more than 700 million. The Soviet Union ranks third, and the United States is close behind. The following table shows the populations of the seven most populous countries according to 1983 estimates.

MOST POPULOUS COUNTRIES IN THE WORLD

Country	Population
1. China	1,015,290,000
2. India	713,006,000
3. Soviet Union	272,535,000
4. United States	230,891,000
5. Indonesia	155,280,000
6. Brazil	126,457,000
7. Japan	119,443,000

Most other countries are much smaller than the United States in population. Three countries have fewer than 10,000 people: the Vatican, Nauru, and Tuvalu.

What does the United States look like?

If you could look down at the United States from a space ship, you would see that the forty-eight connected states are bordered by oceans on the east and the west. The ocean on the west is the Pacific, and the ocean on the east is the Atlantic. Another large body of water lies along the southeast—the Gulf of Mexico. You would clearly see a long peninsula pointing south between the Gulf of Mexico and the Atlantic Ocean. The peninsula is part of the state of Florida.

Farther north you would see five huge lakes connected to one another by rivers or narrow stretches of water called *straits*. These are the Great Lakes, and all but one of them form part of the border between the United States on the south and Canada on the north. From your space ship, you would not be able to see the rest of the Canadian border because it is an imaginary line that shows up only on maps.

If you were close enough to see rivers, you might spot one that flows into the Gulf of Mexico from the west after making a big curve or bend. That is the Rio Grande, the river that forms part of the border between the United States on the north and Mexico on the south.

Far to the north and west of the main part of the United States, you would see a huge peninsula sticking out into the cold North

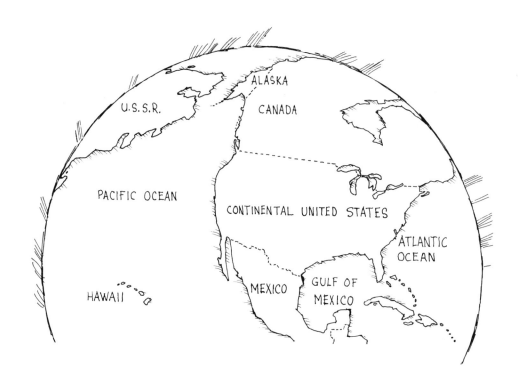

Pacific with a "tail" of islands stretching out to the west. That huge peninsula is the state of Alaska. Even farther to the south and west of the mainland, you might see a collection of small islands far out in the Pacific. These are the Hawaiian Islands and make up the state of Hawaii.

What kinds of land does the United States have?

The United States has almost every kind of land there is in the whole world. Somewhere in the fifty states there are frozen wastelands, deserts, rich farmland, high mountains, volcanoes, rain forests, sandy beaches, rocky coastlines, giant rivers, and much more.

Most of the United States is in a part of the world called the Temperate Zone. This means that it is about halfway between the equator (where the weather is warmest most of the time) and the North Pole (where the weather is coldest most of the time). In the Temperate Zone there are seasons in the year, and the weather ranges from moderately hot to moderately cold.

What countries does the United States border?

The United States has long borders with only two countries: Canada and Mexico. Its whole northern border is with Canada. That border is nearly 4,000 miles long. Alaska also has a long border with Canada. To the southwest, there is a border of some 2,000 miles with Mexico. Canada and Mexico are our two main neighbors.

What other countries are close to the United States?

The closest neighbor to the United States after Mexico and Canada is the Soviet Union. At the far northwestern point of Alaska, the United States and the Soviet Union have islands that are less than

2 miles apart. The mainlands of Alaska and the Soviet Union are about 17 miles apart, separated by the Bering Strait. Very few people live near the border because it is so cold and barren in that part of the world.

In the Southeast, off the shores of Florida, the small island country called the Bahamas lies just to the southeast. The larger country of Cuba is only 80 miles to the south across the Caribbean Sea. Other nearby Caribbean islands are Hispaniola, which is made up of Haiti and the Dominican Republic, Jamaica, and Puerto Rico, which is a territory of the United States.

What is the northernmost point in the United States?

Point Barrow, Alaska, far above the Arctic Circle, facing the Arctic Ocean.

What is the southernmost point in the United States?

The South Cape of the island of Hawaii.

What is the westernmost point in the United States?

The "tail" of islands called the Aleutians, which are part of the state of Alaska, are farther west than any other part of the country. The tiny island of Attu is actually farther west than parts of the Soviet Union. If you sailed directly south from Attu, you would reach New Zealand.

What is the easternmost point in the United States?

The point farthest east has the odd name of West Quoddy Head, Maine.

What is the geographical center of the United States?

If all the land of the United States were paper-thin and in one piece, it could be balanced on one point. Geographers have determined where that point would be. It is near the small town of Castle Rock near the western border of South Dakota.

The geographical center of the forty-eight connected states is near the town of Lebanon in north central Kansas.

What is the population center of the United States?

If each person in the United States weighed the same amount and stood where he or she lives on a giant weightless sheet the shape of the United States, the whole sheet could be balanced on one point. In 1980 that point was in Missouri, just west of the Mississippi River and a few miles south of St. Louis.

The population center changes as people move from one region or state to another. In 1790 the population of the original states centered on a point in Chesapeake Bay in Maryland. Each census since then, it has moved farther west as more and more people moved west to settle the land. By 1860, the population center was in southern Ohio, and by 1890 it was in southern Indiana. Between 1950 and 1970 it was in Illinois, and in 1980 it had crossed the Mississippi River into Missouri.

How did this country get its name?

The name America comes from the name of the explorer Amerigo Vespucci, who sailed along the Atlantic Coast of North America in the early 1500s. When he returned to Europe, mapmakers began putting his name on the newly discovered lands across the Atlantic.

In the 1770s, thirteen separate colonies along the Atlantic shore of America went to war to become independent of Great Britain. They banded together to fight the war. After the war, the colonies decided to stick together and form a single nation. When they gathered to write a Constitution for this nation in 1787, they began with these words: "We the people of *the United States of America* . . ." That became the official name of the country.

Does everyone call the country the United States?

No. Many other people have translated the name United States into their own languages. Thus the United States is known by the following names, among others:

> IN GERMAN: *Die Vereinigten Staaten* (dee Fair-I-nig-ten SHTAH-ten)
> IN FRENCH: *Les Etats-Unis* (layz ay-TAHZ u-NEE)
> IN SPANISH: *Los Estados Unidos* (lohs es-TAH-dohs oo-NEE-dohs)

Many people use the abbreviation U.S.A. as a name for the United States, but they may not pronounce it the way we would. Many would pronounce it OO-ESS-AH.

2

States and Cities

How is the United States divided?

The most important divisions are the states. When the United States was first begun, the representatives of the first thirteen states agreed to form a single government for the whole country. But they also wanted the states to keep many responsibilities of their own. Today there are fifty states, stretching from the Atlantic to the Pacific. Each state has its own governor and makes many of its own laws.

There is one part of the United States that is not in any state. It is called the District of Columbia and consists of the city of Washington, D.C., the capital city of the United States. For many years, it could not make its own laws and was governed by the Congress of the United States. Today it has its own mayor and makes many of its own laws.

Do all the states have the same amount of land?

No. The states vary greatly in size. Some are not much larger than a large city. Others are so large that it would take several days of driving to get from one side to the other.

Which state is largest in area?

In size, the largest state by far is Alaska. It covers nearly 570,000 square miles and stretches nearly 1,500 miles from north to south and some 800 miles from east to west. Much of Alaska's land is frozen wilderness, and nearly all of its people live on a narrow strip of land along the coast of the Pacific Ocean.

The second largest state is Texas, with 262,000 square miles. For more than a hundred years, Texas was the largest, because Alaska didn't become a state until 1959. But now there is room for *two* Texases in Alaska! The third largest state is California, with 156,000 square miles.

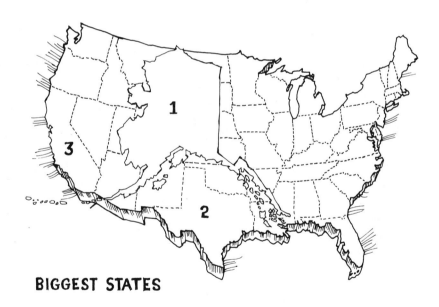

BIGGEST STATES

Which state is smallest in area?

The smallest state is Rhode Island, which has only about 1,050 square miles. It is 40 miles wide from east to west and 30 miles long from north to south. It would fit into Alaska more than five hundred times—yet it has more than twice as many people.

The second and third smallest states are Delaware, with about 2,000 square miles, and Connecticut, with about 5,000.

The District of Columbia is much smaller than any state, covering only 61 square miles. It would fit in a square only 8 miles on a side.

Which state has the most people?

The state with the largest population is California, which had 23.7 million people in 1980. Every ten years, in years that end in zero, the U.S. government takes a *census* to determine the populations of every state. California had the largest population for the first time in 1970.

The state with the second largest population is New York, which had 17.6 million people in 1980. New York had more people than any other state from 1810 through 1960.

Four other states had more than 10 million people in 1980. They are Texas, Pennsylvania, Illinois, and Ohio.

Which state has the fewest people?

The state with the fewest people is also the state with the largest area—Alaska. In 1980 it had just over 400,000 people. For every person who lived in Alaska, there were 58 living in California.

Three other states had fewer than 600,000 people. They are Wyoming, Vermont, and Delaware.

How much land does your state have?

You can find the area of your state on the following table. It gives the states in order from the largest to the smallest. The areas given include only land, not inland water area.

AREA OF THE STATES

State	Area (square miles)	State	Area (square miles)
1. Alaska	569,600	27. Arkansas	51,945
2. Texas	262,134	28. Alabama	50,708
3. California	156,361	29. North Carolina	48,798
4. Montana	145,587	30. New York	47,831
5. New Mexico	121,412	31. Mississippi	47,296
6. Arizona	113,417	32. Pennsylvania	44,966
7. Nevada	109,889	33. Louisiana	44,930
8. Colorado	103,766	34. Tennessee	41,328
9. Wyoming	97,203	35. Ohio	40,975
10. Oregon	96,184	36. Virginia	39,780
11. Idaho	82,677	37. Kentucky	39,650
12. Utah	82,096	38. Indiana	36,097
13. Kansas	81,787	39. Maine	30,920
14. Minnesota	79,289	40. South Carolina	30,225
15. Nebraska	76,483	41. West Virginia	24,070
16. South Dakota	75,955	42. Maryland	9,891
17. North Dakota	69,273	43. Vermont	9,267
18. Missouri	68,995	44. New Hampshire	9,027
19. Oklahoma	68,782	45. Massachusetts	7,826
20. Washington	66,570	46. New Jersey	7,521
21. Georgia	58,073	47. Hawaii	6,425
22. Michigan	56,817	48. Connecticut	4,862
23. Iowa	55,941	49. Delaware	1,982
24. Illinois	55,748	50. Rhode Island	1,049
25. Wisconsin	54,464	51. Dist. Columbia	61
26. Florida	54,090		

How many people does your state have?

The following table shows the populations of all the states according to the 1980 census. It lists all the states in order from the largest to the smallest. See if you can find yours.

POPULATION OF THE STATES

State	Population	State	Population
1. California	23,668,000	27. Iowa	2,914,000
2. New York	17,558,000	28. Colorado	2,890,000
3. Texas	14,229,000	29. Arizona	2,718,000
4. Pennsylvania	11,864,000	30. Oregon	2,633,000
5. Illinois	11,427,000	31. Mississippi	2,521,000
6. Ohio	10,798,000	32. Kansas	2,364,000
7. Florida	9,746,000	33. Arkansas	2,286,000
8. Michigan	9,262,000	34. West Virginia	1,950,000
9. New Jersey	7,365,000	35. Nebraska	1,570,000
10. North Carolina	5,882,000	36. Utah	1,461,000
11. Massachusetts	5,737,000	37. New Mexico	1,303,000
12. Indiana	5,490,000	38. Maine	1,125,000
13. Georgia	5,463,000	39. Hawaii	965,000
14. Virginia	5,347,000	40. Rhode Island	947,000
15. Missouri	4,917,000	41. Idaho	944,000
16. Wisconsin	4,706,000	42. New Hampshire	921,000
17. Tennessee	4,591,000	43. Nevada	800,000
18. Maryland	4,217,000	44. Montana	787,000
19. Louisiana	4,206,000	45. South Dakota	691,000
20. Washington	4,132,000	46. North Dakota	653,000
21. Minnesota	4,076,000	47. Dist. Columbia	638,000
22. Alabama	3,894,000	48. Delaware	594,000
23. Kentucky	3,661,000	49. Vermont	511,000
24. South Carolina	3,122,000	50. Wyoming	470,000
25. Connecticut	3,108,000	51. Alaska	402,000
26. Oklahoma	3,025,000		

Which state is most densely populated?

Density is measured in people per square mile. For example, if a state has 1,000,000 people and 100,000 square miles, it has 10 people for each square mile. The number tells us how crowded or uncrowded a state is. The whole United States has a density of 63.9 people per square mile.

The most densely populated state is New Jersey, which has a fairly large population and quite a small area. In New Jersey there are 986.2 people per square mile.

The District of Columbia, which had 638,000 people in 1980 on only 61 square miles, has 10,132 people per square mile.

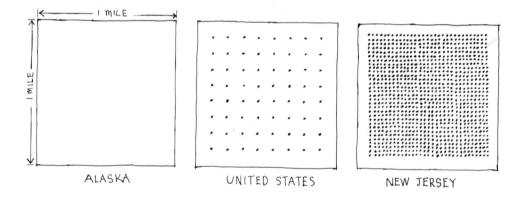

PEOPLE PER SQUARE MILE
(EACH DOT EQUALS ONE PERSON)

Which state is least densely populated?

One state, Alaska, actually has more square miles than it has people. Alaska has 569,600 square miles and only 402,000 people. So its density is 0.7 people per square mile.

How many states have an ocean shoreline?

Twenty-three of the fifty touch the ocean, and some have very long shorelines. They are:

Pacific shoreline: Hawaii, Alaska, Washington, Oregon, California

Gulf of Mexico shoreline: Texas, Louisiana, Mississippi, Alabama

Gulf of Mexico and Atlantic shoreline: Florida

Atlantic shoreline: Georgia, South Carolina, North Carolina, Virginia, Maryland, Delaware, New Jersey, New York, Connecticut, Rhode Island, Massachusetts, New Hampshire, Maine

Which states have the fewest borders with other states?

Alaska and Hawaii have no borders with other states. Among the forty-eight connected states, Maine is the only one that has a border with just one other state. The rest of its borders are with Canada and the Atlantic Ocean.

In one place you can lie down so that parts of your body are in four states at once. Where is that place?

It is a point called the Four Corners, where the corners of Arizona, Utah, Colorado and New Mexico meet. This is the only place where four states come together.

Which states have large islands?

Hawaii is made up entirely of islands. The most important are Oahu, where most of the people live, and Hawaii, which is the largest of the chain. All together, there are several hundred islands in the group, but many of them are small, and no one lives on them.

Alaska also has many islands. In fact, many of its towns are on islands and can be reached only by ship or plane.

The most densely populated island in the United States is Long Island in New York State. It is 90 miles long and has more than 6,700,000 people.

What is a state capital?

A state capital is a town or city where the state government does its business. The state legislature meets there, and the governor has his or her offices there.

Is the state capital always the largest city in a state?

No. In fact, most of the largest cities in the United States are *not* state capitals.

What are the largest state capitals?

There are four capitals with more than 500,000 people. They are Phoenix, Arizona (789,704); Indianapolis, Indiana (700,807); Columbus, Ohio (565,032); and Boston, Massachusetts (562,994).

What are the smallest state capitals?

The smallest is Montpelier, Vermont, which has only 8,241 people. Two other capitals have fewer than 20,000 people. They are Pierre, South Dakota (11,973); and Juneau, Alaska (19,528).

What state capital can't be reached by road from the rest of its state?

Juneau, Alaska. The town is surrounded by glaciers, mountains, and water. Visitors must come by boat or airplane.

What is your state capital?

You can find the capital of your state and its population on the following table.

CAPITALS OF THE STATES

State	Capital	Capital Population
Alabama	Montgomery	177,857
Alaska	Juneau	19,528
Arizona	Phoenix	789,704
Arkansas	Little Rock	158,915
California	Sacramento	275,741
Colorado	Denver	492,365
Connecticut	Hartford	136,392
Delaware	Dover	23,507
Florida	Tallahassee	81,548
Georgia	Atlanta	425,022
Hawaii	Honolulu	365,048
Idaho	Boise	102,160
Illinois	Springfield	100,054
Indiana	Indianapolis	700,807
Iowa	Des Moines	191,003
Kansas	Topeka	115,266
Kentucky	Frankfort	25,973
Louisiana	Baton Rouge	219,844
Maine	Augusta	21,819
Maryland	Annapolis	31,740
Massachusetts	Boston	562,994
Michigan	Lansing	130,414
Minnesota	St. Paul	270,230
Mississippi	Jackson	202,895
Missouri	Jefferson City	33,619

CAPITALS OF THE STATES

State	Capital	Capital Population
Montana	Helena	23,938
Nebraska	Lincoln	171,932
Nevada	Carson City	32,022
New Hampshire	Concord	30,400
New Jersey	Trenton	92,124
New Mexico	Santa Fe	48,953
New York	Albany	101,727
North Carolina	Raleigh	150,255
North Dakota	Bismarck	44,485
Ohio	Columbus	565,032
Oklahoma	Oklahoma City	403,484
Oregon	Salem	89,233
Pennsylvania	Harrisburg	53,264
Rhode Island	Providence	156,804
South Carolina	Columbia	101,229
South Dakota	Pierre	11,973
Tennessee	Nashville	455,651
Texas	Austin	435,890
Utah	Salt Lake City	163,034
Vermont	Montpelier	8,241
Virginia	Richmond	219,214
Washington	Olympia	27,447
West Virginia	Charleston	63,968
Wisconsin	Madison	170,618
Wyoming	Cheyenne	47,283

What are the regions of the United States?

There are many ways to break the country into regions. Most people recognize four great regions, which we call the Northeast, the South, the Midwest, and the West.

What states are in the Northeast?

The Northeast has the smallest area of the four regions. Nine states are tucked into the northeastern corner of the country. The six states farthest north are often called New England. They are Maine,

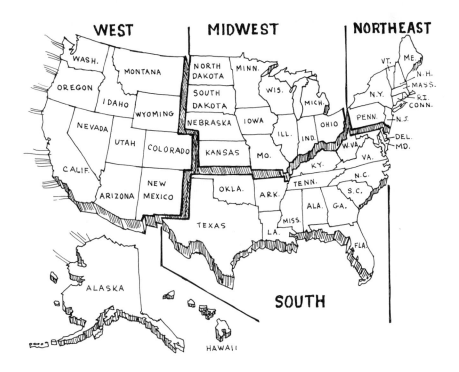

New Hampshire, Vermont, Massachusetts, Rhode Island, and Connecticut. The major city in New England is Boston.

The southern half of the Northeast region is taken up by three states, sometimes called the Middle Atlantic states. They are New York, New Jersey, and Pennsylvania. New York and Philadelphia are the largest cities in this part of the Northeast.

In 1980 the Northeast had about 50 million people, making it the third largest of the four regions in population. Since it also has the smallest area, however, it is the most densely populated region, with 302 people per square mile.

What states are in the South?

The South has sixteen states and the District of Columbia. We can divide the states into four groups with four states in each group.

The first group of states is clustered around Chesapeake Bay. These states are Virginia, Maryland, Delaware, and West Virginia. Until 1863 West Virginia was not a state at all, but a part of Virginia. The District of Columbia, which is the city of Washington, the capital of the United States, is a small piece of land between Virginia and Maryland. Many government employees who work in Washington, D.C., live in Virginia or Maryland.

The second group lies south of Virginia along the Atlantic Coast. It includes North Carolina, South Carolina, Georgia, and Florida.

The third group is west of the Appalachian Mountains and east of the Mississippi River. It consists of Kentucky, Tennessee, Alabama, and Mississippi.

The final group of southern states is the farthest west, stretching from the Mississippi River almost to the Rocky Mountains. The states in this group are Louisiana, Arkansas, Texas, and Oklahoma.

In 1980 the South had about 75 million people, making it the most populous of the four regions. One American in three lives in the South. It is the second most densely populated region with about 86 people per square mile.

What states are in the Midwest?

There are twelve midwestern states, and they can be divided into two groups, eastern and western.

The eastern group is clustered around the Great Lakes and lies east of the Mississippi River. This group includes Ohio, Indiana, Illinois, Michigan, and Wisconsin.

The western group is best known for its farms. Missouri, Iowa, and Minnesota lie just to the west of the Mississippi. Farther west are Kansas, Nebraska, South Dakota, and North Dakota.

The Midwest has nearly 60 million people, making it the second most populous of the regions. It is third most densely populated, with 78 people per square mile.

What states are in the West?

The thirteen western states can be broken into two groups. The first is called the Mountain Region because the rugged Rocky Mountains run through it. The eight mountain states have large areas and small populations. They are New Mexico and Arizona in the south; Colorado, Wyoming, Utah, and Nevada in the center; and Montana and Idaho in the north.

The second group of western states lies along the Pacific Ocean. It includes California, Oregon, Washington, and the two "disconnected" states of Alaska and Hawaii.

The western region has 43 million people, making it the least populous of the four regions. It is also the least densely populated with only 25 people per square mile. It is the largest region in area; in fact, it has almost half the land in the United States.

Do all the regions grow at the same rate?

No. Between 1970 and 1980 the populations of the South and the West increased rapidly. These two regions together gained more than 21 million people. The Northeast and Midwest together gained only 3 million.

Why do the regions grow at different rates?

The main reason is that people have been moving from the Northeast and Midwest to the South and the West. In the 1970s and 1980s many people in the Northeast and Midwest couldn't find jobs there, so they moved to the South or the West. There are many new industries in the growing regions, and people also like the warmer winters.

What is the Sunbelt?

The Sunbelt is made up of the states along the southern edge of
the United States from Florida in the east to southern California in
the west. This group of states includes all three of the states that
gained the most people in the 1970s: California, Texas, and
Florida.

Sometimes the Sunbelt is compared to another group of states
called the Snowbelt—those states along the northern border of the
United States from Maine to Washington. Those states are not
gaining population rapidly. In fact, between 1970 and 1980 two of
them—New York and Rhode Island—actually lost population.

What are the largest cities in the United States?

That is a hard question to answer. If we count only the population
inside the city's limits, the largest cities in 1980 are shown below:

1. New York, New York   7,071,000
2. Chicago, Illinois   3,005,000
3. Los Angeles, California   2,967,000
4. Philadelphia, Pennsylvania 1,688,000
5. Houston, Texas   1,594,000

But many cities have odd city limits; and many of the people who
work and shop in them live in nearby towns called suburbs. So in
order to measure the size of cities more accurately, we now talk
about "metropolitan areas."

What is a metropolitan area?

A metropolitan area is a group of cities and towns that make a
natural cluster. One metropolitan area may have as many as sixty
towns and cities. But people there usually have many things in
common. They watch the same television stations, listen to the

same radio stations, shop at the same chain of markets, and root for the same home teams in sports.

The U.S. Bureau of the Census studies clusters of towns and defines the metropolitan areas.

How many metropolitan areas are there?

The U.S. Census Bureau has identified 323 standard metropolitan areas. Of these, 38 had more than 1,000,000 people. All of them had more than 100,000.

In 1980 three out of four Americans lived in the 323 metropolitan areas—in a cluster of towns and cities with a population of more than 100,000. Together, the metropolitan areas had a population of 169 million. The total of people living outside metropolitan areas was 57 million.

What are the largest metropolitan areas?

The five largest metropolitan areas are:

1. New York City–New Jersey	9,120,000
2. Los Angeles–Long Beach, California	7,478,000
3. Chicago, Illinois	7,102,000
4. Philadelphia, Pennsylvania–New Jersey	4,717,000
5. Detroit, Michigan	4,353,000

What regions have the most large cities?

The Northeast and the Midwest. There are two long strips or "corridors" of large cities in the United States. One runs along the coast of the Northeast from Boston through New York and Philadelphia and down to Washington, D.C. This corridor holds most of the population of the northeastern region and includes the major cities of Baltimore and Washington in the southern region. It is sometimes called Bos-Wash for the cities at each end.

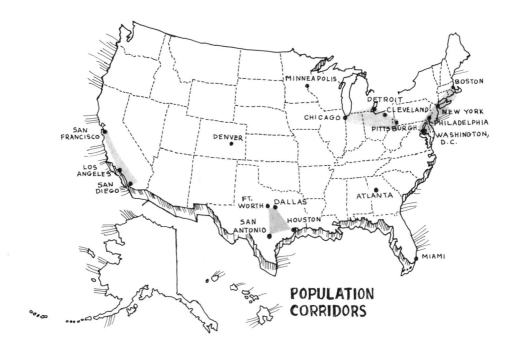

POPULATION CORRIDORS

The second corridor runs along the southern edge of the Great Lakes in the midwestern region from Chicago through Detroit and Cleveland to Pittsburgh, Pennsylvania. It includes a fair proportion of the Midwest's population and connects the Midwest to the northeastern states. Its nickname is Chi-Pitts.

There are smaller corridors of big cities in the West and South. One is growing in California along the Pacific shore from San Francisco south to Los Angeles and San Diego. It is called San-San. Another cluster of very large cities is growing in Texas and includes Houston, Dallas–Forth Worth, and San Antonio.

Other large cities are not in any cluster or corridor. Three such cities are Atlanta, Georgia; Denver, Colorado; and Minneapolis, Minnesota. They are isolated cities that serve as the most important cities in regions covering many states.

3

The Land

What is the highest point in the United States?

The highest point is the peak of Mount McKinley in Alaska, about 125 miles from the city of Anchorage. It is 20,320 feet—or nearly 4 miles—above sea level. Mount McKinley is also the highest place in North America. It is more than a mile higher than any mountain in the forty-eight connected states. A number of other peaks in Alaska are higher than 15,000 feet.

What is the highest point in the forty-eight connected states?

Mount Whitney in California is 14,494 feet above sea level, about 60 feet higher than Mount Elbert in the Colorado Rocky Mountains. There are nearly sixty peaks in Colorado that are between 14,000 and 14,400 feet in altitude.

What are the main mountain systems in the United States?

The largest mountain system is the one we call the Rocky Mountains. It runs from central Alaska through western Canada and

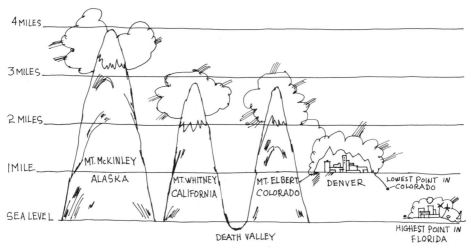

ALTITUDES FROM SEA LEVEL

through the states of Montana, Idaho, Wyoming, Utah, and Colorado, coming to an end in northern New Mexico.

A second important system is the Pacific Range. It runs from southern Alaska through western Canada and through the states of Washington, Oregon, and California. Both Mount McKinley in Alaska and Mount Whitney in California are part of the Pacific system. In the United States, the Great Basin lies between the Rocky and Pacific chains. The basin covers most of Nevada and parts of several other states.

Are there any important mountains in the eastern United States?

Yes. The third great mountain system is the Appalachians, which run from northern New England through eastern New York, Pennsylvania, Virginia, West Virginia, Kentucky, North Carolina, Tennessee, and into northern Alabama. The Appalachians are much older mountains than the Rocky and Pacific ranges and have been gradually worn down. The highest peaks in the Appalachians are less than 7,000 feet above sea level.

What about other mountain ranges?

The Ozark and Ouachita mountains in Arkansas, Oklahoma, and Missouri make up a separate small system with peaks less than 3,000 feet above sea level.

Most other ranges are parts of the large systems listed above. For example, various parts of the Appalachians are called the Cumberland Mountains, the Alleghenies, the Berkshires, the Green Mountains, and so on. Various parts of the Rocky and Pacific mountain chains also have different names.

What is the Continental Divide?

The Continental Divide is an imaginary line that runs down the middle of the Rocky Mountains. Any rain that falls to the west of the line will find its way westward to the Pacific Ocean. Any rain that falls to the east of the line will find its way eastward to the Gulf of Mexico, which is a part of the Atlantic Ocean.

A similar imaginary line runs through the Appalachian Mountains. Water falling to the east of that line will flow eastward to the Atlantic, and water falling to the west of the line will flow west and south toward the Gulf of Mexico.

What is the lowest point in the United States?

The lowest place is Death Valley in California, which reaches 282 feet below sea level. Death Valley is part of a huge desert and has some of the hottest and driest weather in North America. Only 75 miles away is Mount Whitney, towering more than 14,000 feet above sea level. A hike from the bottom of Death Valley to the top of Mount Whitney is probably the steepest uphill walk in America.

What are the highest and lowest states?

The highest state is Colorado. Its *lowest* point is more than 3,000 feet above sea level. Its major city, Denver, is known as the Mile High City because of its altitude of about 5,280 feet. And there are hundreds of mountain peaks in Colorado that are more than two miles high.

The lowest state is Florida. Its *highest* point is only 350 feet above sea level, and much of the state is only a few feet above sea level.

What is the largest body of water in the United States?

The largest lake entirely in the United States is Lake Michigan, one of the five Great Lakes, with an area of 22,300 square miles. This area makes it about the size of West Virginia—or three times the size of New Jersey.

What are the Great Lakes?

There are five Great Lakes connected to each other by rivers or straits. Together, they make up the largest freshwater lake system in the world, with a water surface of nearly 88,000 square miles. This area is larger than that of any state east of the Mississippi River— and greater than the area of the six New England states together.

One of the Great Lakes, Michigan, is all in the United States. The other four form part of our border with Canada. The actual boundary runs through the middle of the lakes, so about half of their area is in the United States and half in Canada. From west to east, these

THE LAND

lakes are Superior, Huron, Erie, and Ontario. The water in the lakes runs eastward. From Lake Ontario, it flows into the St. Lawrence River, which runs through eastern Canada to the Atlantic Ocean.

Eight states of the United States have shores on the Great Lakes. They are, from west to east, Minnesota, Wisconsin, Illinois, Indiana, Michigan, Ohio, Pennsylvania, and New York.

What is the St. Lawrence Seaway?

In the 1950s, Canada and the United States worked together to develop the St. Lawrence River and the system of locks along the rivers between the other Great Lakes. This huge St. Lawrence

Seaway project allowed ocean-going ships to travel from the Atlantic Ocean into and through the Great Lakes. Barges and tankers carry goods to and from American and Canadian ports on the Great Lakes.

What state touches all but one of the Great Lakes?

Michigan. This state is made up of two peninsulas. The Southern Peninsula is surrounded on three sides by the lakes: Michigan to the west and northwest, Huron to the northeast and east, and Erie in the far southeast.

The Northern Peninsula is sandwiched between Lake Michigan to the south and Lake Superior to the north. The Northern and Southern Peninsulas are separated by the Straits of Mackinac, the narrow stretch of water between Lake Michigan and Lake Huron.

Are there other large lakes in the United States?

There are many other lakes, but none of them is nearly as large as the Great Lakes.

The Great Salt Lake in Utah is interesting because its water is much saltier than that of the oceans. It also varies greatly in size depending on the amount of rain and snowfall in the surrounding mountains. Other large natural lakes include Okeechobee in Florida and Champlain between New York and Vermont.

There are also many large man-made lakes, that were created by placing dams across great rivers. Among the largest are Franklin D. Roosevelt Lake on the Columbia River behind Grand Coulee Dam in Washington State, and two lakes on the Colorado River: Powell in Utah and Arizona, and Mead in Arizona and Nevada.

What is the largest river system in the United States?

The largest river system by far is the Mississippi. By the time it reaches the Gulf of Mexico, the Mississippi carries water from twenty-seven states. It receives runoff from a funnel-shaped area stretching from the Rocky Mountains to the Appalachians.

The Mississippi River itself is about 2,350 miles long. It begins at Lake Itasca in Northern Minnesota and flows into the Gulf of Mexico near New Orleans, Louisiana. For most of its length, the Mississippi serves as a border between states, so its course can be seen on any map with state outlines. On its western shore are most of Minnesota, all of Iowa, Missouri, and Arkansas, and most of Louisiana. On its eastern shore are Wisconsin, Illinois, Kentucky, Tennessee, and Mississippi.

What other large rivers are part of the Mississippi system?

The two largest rivers that flow into the Mississippi are the Missouri and the Ohio. The Missouri begins in the Rocky Mountains in western Montana and covers more than 2,300 miles before flowing into the Mississippi near St. Louis, Missouri.

The Ohio begins at Pittsburgh, Pennsylvania, where it is formed by the meeting of the Allegheny and Monongahela rivers. Like the Mississippi, the Ohio forms an important border between states. On its northern shore are Ohio, Indiana, and Illinois, and on its southern shore are West Virginia and Kentucky.

Are there other important river systems in the United States?

Yes. The St. Lawrence River, which receives water from the Great Lakes and from tributary rivers in Canada and the United States, is the second most important.

The Columbia River and its tributaries in the Northwest have been dammed to produce huge amounts of electricity. The Colorado River and its tributaries in the Southwest have been dammed both to make electricity and to provide water to irrigate desert lands. The Rio Grande (which means Great River) is another southwestern river that serves as the boundary between Texas and Mexico.

Are there major rivers in the East?

Yes, but they are not as large as those in the Midwest and West. They include the Connecticut in New England; the Hudson in New York State; the Delaware, which is the main border between Pennsylvania and New Jersey; the Susquehanna; the Potomac, which flows past Washington, D.C.; the James; the Roanoke; the Savannah; and others.

Do all rivers finally end at the sea?

Most rivers do flow to the sea. But some rivers appear to be "dead ends." Pioneers found such rivers in the Great Basin region of the United States between the Rocky and Pacific mountain ranges. In this dry, hot region, millions of gallons of water run off the surrounding mountains into streams and rivers. The settlers eagerly followed the rivers, hoping to find a good source of water and a way through the mountains. But the rivers ended in "sinks"— basins where most of the water evaporated in the hot sun, leaving only salt and other chemicals. The remaining water was poisoned by the chemicals.

What is a prairie?

When settlers first saw the Midwest, they were amazed to find country with rolling hills and very few trees. Instead of trees, thick grasses grew more than five feet tall as far as the eye could see. The settlers discovered that the soil there was black and rich and that hot, humid summers were good for raising grain. These prairie lands, covering much of Illinois and Iowa and parts of surrounding states, became the most productive farmland in the world. Today, instead of prairie grasses, the rich soil produces corn, soybeans, and other crops that help feed millions.

Farther west, the country became ever flatter, and the grasses grew only two or three feet high. This region the settlers called the Great Plains. These plains stretch from Texas in the south through the Dakotas in the north and far north into Canada. The soil is fertile here, too, but there is less rain. Soon the Great Plains were the greatest wheat producer the world, providing flour and other grain products and feed for livestock.

Together the prairies and the plains are the great food basket of America.

Are there deserts in the United States?

Usually we think of a desert as a place that has no water, little or no rain, and very hot weather. A large region of the southwestern United States fits this description. It includes a large area in southern California and parts of Nevada, Utah, Arizona, and New Mexico. This desert region includes Death Valley, the lowest place in North America, and a nearby desert called the Mojave (mo-HAH-vee).

The least inviting desert in the United States is the Great Salt Lake Desert in Utah near the Great Salt Lake. This desert is covered with a hard white sheet of salt. The desert is blinding in the bright sunlight, and of course any water you might find there would be too salty to drink. The only use for this desert is to conduct speed-racing tests. World land speed records of more than 600 miles per hour have been set by rocket cars on the flat salt floor of the Great Salt Lake Desert.

Are there any jungles in the United States?

"Jungle" is a name most often given to a *tropical rain forest*. Such forests have a variety of plant and animal life, but are not very healthful for people to live in. There are no real tropical rain forests in the United States.

Parts of southern Florida are almost tropical, however. The Everglades and other swamplands have thick, tangled plant life—and alligators live in the shallow waters. These swamplands are a kind of jungle, but they are very different from the rain forests of South America and Africa.

Does the United States have any volcanoes?

Yes. There are many volcanoes in the United States, but most of them are *extinct,* which means that they have not erupted for thousands of years.

Have any volcanoes erupted in recent years?

Yes. On May 18, 1980, Mount St. Helens in southern Washington State erupted violently. At least thirty-four people were killed by the effects of the blast. Trees for dozens of miles around were knocked down, and thousands of tons of volcanic ash were thrown high in the air and blown around the world by high-altitude winds.

Mount St. Helens was the first volcano to erupt in the forty-eight connected states since 1914–17, when Lassen Peak in California erupted.

Are any other volcanoes active now?

Yes. If you are looking for active volcanoes, your best bet is to visit Hawaii. The Hawaiian Islands were formed by volcanoes. The islands are really the tops of very high mountains whose sides are mostly under the sea. Volcanic eruptions have helped add more height to the huge underwater mountains and more area to the islands.

The largest of the islands, Hawaii, has five volcanoes, including the only two in the state that are still active—Mauna Loa and

Kilauea. Visitors can drive almost to the edge of Kilauea and see the fiery liquid rock called lava. During 1983 Kilauea sent a stream of lava down one of its sides that threatened a village with destruction. In 1984 Mauna Loa also erupted, and new flows of lava came to the outskirts of the city of Hilo.

What was the largest volcanic eruption in the United States?

The largest eruption in recorded history was that of Novarupta on the Alaskan Peninsula in 1912. The whole top of nearby Mount Katmai collapsed, forming a huge crater called a caldera nearly 4,000 feet deep and three miles across. The Valley of Ten Thousand Smokes was formed nearby where steam and hot gases still escape from holes in the ground.

There are many active volcanoes on the Aleutian Islands, which stretch westward from Alaska. Mount Wrangell, on the Alaskan mainland, is also classified as active.

What parts of the United States have had earthquakes?

Almost every region of the United States has experienced earthquakes at some time or other. One of the largest on record was in the Mississippi Valley in 1811. The force of the earthquake changed the course of the great river and created a lake where the river used to flow. The region was not settled at that time, however, so damage to man-made things was slight.

Are there more earthquakes in some areas than in others?

Yes. A narrow band of earthquake territory runs along the shore of the Pacific Ocean from southern California all the way through western Canada, Alaska, and the Aleutian Islands. This is the same part of the country that has the most volcanoes.

Earthquakes often happen along breaks in the earth called *faults,* and one of the largest of these, the San Andreas Fault, runs from San Francisco southeast into central and southern California. The most damaging earthquake in American history happened in 1906 near San Francisco. That city was damaged by the earthquake and largely destroyed by the fire that followed. The earthquake broke gas mains, which fed the fires. About seven hundred people were killed. Other smaller quakes happen in California every few years, and scientists say that one day there may be another large, destructive one.

More recently, in 1964, a giant earthquake struck the Alaskan coast between Anchorage and Valdez. About 130 people were killed.

What is a glacier?

A glacier is a huge sheet of ice that moves slowly across the land or down a mountain valley. *Continental glaciers* are so huge that they move in all directions from their center and can cover huge areas of land. *Valley glaciers* are much smaller, but their power is still amazing.

Are there any continental glaciers in the United States?

Not now. But during the last ice age, huge continental glaciers pushed their way down from the North Pole into much of the Midwest and Northeast. Geologists still find traces of the glaciers' work, since they were powerful enough to move huge boulders and thousands of tons of smaller rock. When the glaciers melted, these rocks were left where they had been "dropped" by the ice. The only continental glaciers today are in Antarctica and Greenland.

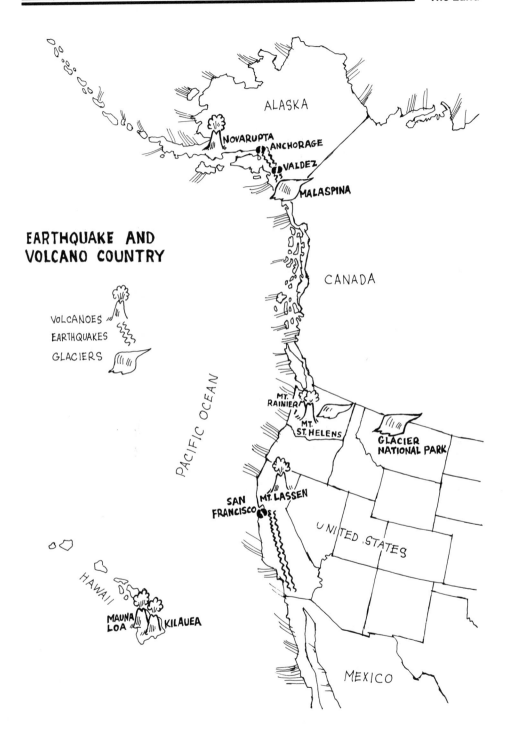

EARTHQUAKE AND
VOLCANO COUNTRY

VOLCANOES
EARTHQUAKES
GLACIERS

ALASKA

NOVARUPTA
ANCHORAGE
VALDEZ
MALASPINA

CANADA

PACIFIC OCEAN

MT. RAINIER
MT. ST. HELENS
GLACIER NATIONAL PARK

SAN FRANCISCO
MT. LASSEN

UNITED STATES

HAWAII
MAUNA LOA
KILAUEA

MEXICO

Are there any mountain glaciers in the United States?

Yes. There are glaciers in Glacier National Park on the border between Montana and Canada and on the sides of Mount Rainier in Washington. In addition, there are more than a thousand mountain glaciers in Alaska. The largest of these is called Malaspina and is an ice sheet 50 miles across. Many Alaskan glaciers are easy to visit and attract many tourists. They move only a few feet a day and can be watched and studied safely.

4
Weather

What kind of climate does the United States have?

The United States is so large and stretches so far that it has many kinds of climate. The weather in northern Alaska is arctic, and the weather in Hawaii is tropical. The forty-eight connected states also have many different kinds of weather.

What is the coldest place in America?

In January 1971 a temperature of 79.8 degrees below zero Fahrenheit was measured at Prospect Creek Camp in Alaska. This is probably the lowest temperature ever recorded in the United States. The lowest temperature ever recorded anywhere was at a Soviet station in Antarctica: 127 degrees below zero Fahrenheit.

Not all of Alaska is bitter cold, however. On an average January day, Juneau, Alaska, is actually warmer than cities in Minnesota or the Dakotas.

Temperatures below zero have been recorded at least once in every state except Hawaii, where the record low temperature is 14 degrees Fahrenheit.

What is the coldest town in the United States?

By all measurements, the champion is Barrow, Alaska. Barrow's temperature falls below zero on almost half the days of the year and has freezing temperatures (32 degrees or below Fahrenheit) all but forty days a year.

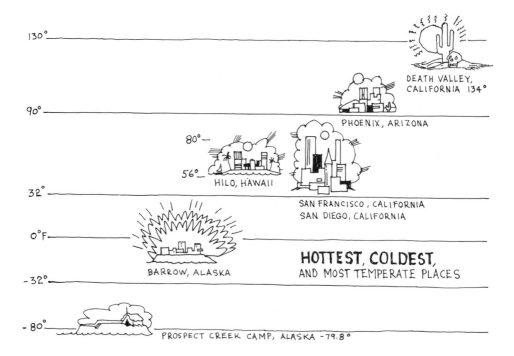

130°

90°

80° —

56° —

32°

0°F

-32°

- 80°

DEATH VALLEY, CALIFORNIA 134°

PHOENIX, ARIZONA

HILO, HAWAII

SAN FRANCISCO, CALIFORNIA
SAN DIEGO, CALIFORNIA

BARROW, ALASKA

HOTTEST, COLDEST, AND MOST TEMPERATE PLACES

PROSPECT CREEK CAMP, ALASKA -79.8°

What is the hottest place in the United States?

The hottest temperature ever recorded under controlled conditions was registered in 1913 in California's Death Valley—134 degrees Fahrenheit. This is only two degrees below the world record of 136 degrees recorded in the Sahara Desert of North Africa. Death Valley's average twenty-four-hour temperature in the summer is above 98 degrees.

Every state, even Alaska, has recorded a temperature of 100 or higher at least once.

What is the hottest city in the United States?

Phoenix, Arizona, records 169 days each year when the temperature is 90 degrees or higher. This gives it more hot days than any other city in the United States. Only 300 miles away in Flagstaff, Arizona, the temperature gets to 90 only about three days a year, but it goes below freezing on two hundred days.

What are the most temperate cities in the United States?

A temperate climate is one that never gets too hot or too cold. In Hilo, Hawaii, in an average year, the temperature will never get to 90 degrees Fahrenheit and will never drop as low as 32. In fact, the lowest temperature ever recorded there is 56 degrees.

In the forty-eight connected states, the most temperate cities are San Francisco and San Diego, California. Both cities can expect only seven days a year when the temperature will reach 90 degrees Fahrenheit or go below freezing.

What is the wettest place in the United States?

The wettest spot in the United States—and probably on all the earth—is Mount Waialeale on the Hawaiian island of Kauai. It receives an average of 460 inches of rain—more than 38 feet!—each year. On the average, it rains 1.25 inches every day. Most of the rain in the Hawaiian Islands is caught by the mountains. Honolulu, the capital of Hawaii, receives only about 23 inches of rain a year.

In the forty-eight connected states, the wettest place is the Olympic Peninsula in Washington State, which averages more than 130 inches of rain a year. Seattle, only 50 miles away, receives only 39 inches.

The major cities that receive the most rain are those in the southeastern states. Mobile, Alabama, averages 67 inches per year.

How much is one inch of rain?

Rainfall is usually measured by a gauge in a very limited area. But one inch of rain falling over an area of one acre (a square 208 feet on a side) measures more than 27,000 gallons. Since there are 640 acres in a square mile, one inch of rain over one square mile requires 17,300,000 gallons of water.

What is the snowiest place in the United States?

The largest snowfall for a year (from July through June) was recorded on the slopes of Mount Rainier in Washington State. In 1971–72, the ranger station on the mountain recorded 1,122 inches (93½ feet) of snow.

Other mountain areas in the Pacific and Rocky mountains hold other records. For example, a fall of 76 inches in one 24-hour period was recorded in Silver Lake, Colorado, in 1921. And Tamarack, California, recorded 390 inches (32½ feet) in the month of January 1911.

Outside of mountain regions, the largest average snowfalls occur in New York State just south of Lake Ontario and in parts of Ohio and Pennsylvania south of Lake Erie. Many communities in these snow belts average 150 inches of snow each winter.

How much is an inch of snow?

Since snow is much less dense than rain, an inch of snow does not have nearly as much moisture as an inch of rain. If the snow is very dry, it may take 30 inches to equal one inch of rain. If the snow is very moist, 6 inches will equal an inch of rain.

What is the driest place in the United States?

Death Valley is the winner again. On the average, it receives 1.63 inches of rain a year, less than any other place where regular weather records are kept. The settlement of Bagdad, California, recorded a stretch of 767 days without a trace of rain from 1912 to 1914.

The driest state is Nevada, which gets about 7 inches of rain a year.

Where is the sunniest place in the United States?

Among large towns and cities, the two with the most sunny days each year are Las Vegas, Nevada, with 225 days, and Yuma, Arizona, with 222 days. Both places can be very hot in the summer and have little rain.

Where is the cloudiest place in the United States?

The place with the most overcast days is Portland, Oregon, with 248 each year—about two days out of every three. Other cloudy cities include several in Oregon and Washington and Buffalo and Rochester, New York.

Where is the windiest place in the United States?

The most amazing records for wind belong to a weather station on top of Mount Washington in New Hampshire. Over many years, the average wind speed there has been 35 miles per hour.

Mount Washington also recorded the greatest wind speed in the United States during a storm in the 1930s. The wind blew steadily

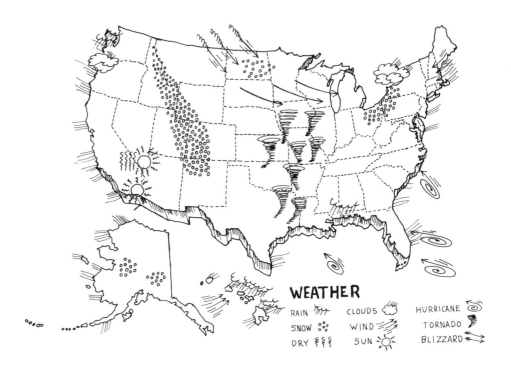

WEATHER

RAIN	CLOUDS	HURRICANE
SNOW	WIND	TORNADO
DRY	SUN	BLIZZARD

at about 188 miles per hour for five minutes. Then came a gust that registered 231 miles per hour. Shortly afterward the measuring device was blown from its moorings and wrecked.

What is the most dangerous kind of storm in the United States?

Many kinds of storms can be dangerous to people and property, but probably the most dangerous of all is the hurricane. A hurricane is a huge storm as much as 400 miles across. Its winds move counterclockwise (if you are looking down on them) at speeds of more than 100 miles per hour. The hurricane often carries heavy rains as well as dangerous winds.

Is Chicago the windiest city in the United States?

No. Although it is called the Windy City, its average winds are not as great as those in Boston, Buffalo, Honolulu, Key West, and a number of other cities.

What parts of the United States get hurricanes?

Hurricanes are "born" between June and November in the Atlantic Ocean near the equator. They come toward North America from the southeast and may strike along the Atlantic Coast of the United States or in Florida and along the rest of the Gulf Coast. Since hurricanes rapidly lose their force when they travel over land, they are most dangerous near the coast. In this century they have struck from New England to Texas.

Where have the worst hurricanes struck?

In 1900 a hurricane hit Galveston, Texas, and killed more than six thousand people. This was probably the greatest loss of life from a hurricane in the United States. Galveston was struck again by Hurricane Alicia in 1983.

Today, weather forecasters, using satellites and radar, can give early warning of approaching hurricanes so that people in low-lying areas near the coast can be evacuated. This saves many lives, but hurricanes can still cause terrible damage to homes and businesses. In 1972 Hurricane Agnes struck the heavily populated areas between North Carolina and New York and caused more than $3 billion in damage.

Do hurricanes strike other parts of the world?

Yes, but they are called by different names. Those rising in the Pacific Ocean are called *typhoons* and those in the Indian Ocean are called *cyclones.* In 1970 a severe cyclone struck the country of Bangladesh, and more than 300,000 people died.

What is a tornado?

A tornado is a local windstorm that may have winds even higher than those in a hurricane. But a tornado is usually only a few hundred yards wide. When it strikes the ground, it can lift whole houses into the air, carry people and livestock from one place to another, and even drive a piece of straw through a solid wood post. About seven hundred tornadoes are reported in the United States each year. They are most common in the spring and early summer.

Where do tornadoes strike?

Tornadoes, or twisters, have been sighted in all states east of the Rocky Mountains, but they are most common in a belt that runs through the south and central states and includes parts of Texas, Oklahoma, Kansas, Nebraska, Missouri, and Iowa. Tornadoes usually come from the southwest. Modern weather forecasting has made it possible to issue tornado alerts whenever a twister is sighted. When weather conditions are right, there may be several tornadoes in the region at the same time.

What were the worst tornadoes?

On March 18, 1925, a tornado swept across Missouri, Illinois, and Indiana and killed nearly seven hundred people. It traveled 220 miles in less than four hours and in some places its path was nearly a mile wide.

In April 1936 a group of tornadoes struck the southern states from Arkansas to South Carolina, and five hundred people were killed. In 1953 and again in 1955 tornadoes in the upper Midwest caused widespread damage and death. And in 1974 tornadoes from Alabama to Ohio killed more than three hundred people.

A tornado can cause enormous damage if it strikes a large town or city. The tornadoes causing the most damage are not necessarily the most powerful; they are the ones that happened to strike where thousands of people were living.

What is a blizzard?

A blizzard is a severe winter storm that brings low temperatures, high winds, and heavy snows. The National Weather Service calls a snowstorm a blizzard when its winds are above 35 miles per hour, its temperatures below 20 degrees Fahrenheit, and when visibility is reduced to less than one quarter of a mile. If the storm has higher winds and lower temperatures, and visibility is nearly zero, the Weather Service calls it a "severe blizzard."

Where do blizzards happen?

Blizzards are most common in the northern United States east of the Rocky Mountains. A blizzard occurs when a mass of cold Arctic air sweeps down through the plains of Canada and into the northern United States. The upper Midwest has especially severe winter weather and can expect at least one blizzard each winter. One big danger is getting lost in the swirling snow. In a severe blizzard it is impossible to see more than a few feet in any direction. People can get lost in their own yards.

What were the worst blizzards?

Within two weeks in 1978 two giant blizzards caused widespread damage and suffering in the Midwest and the Northeast. The first of these, on January 26 and 27, was said to be the worst blizzard of the century. Winds of up to 100 miles per hour were recorded, and thousand of travelers were stranded. In February 1973 a blizzard surprised the South and left as much as 20 inches of snow in Georgia and the Carolinas.

The most famous blizzard of the 1800s struck in March 1888. More than 40 inches of snow fell on the Northeast, and more than four hundred people died in the storm.

What is a nor'easter?

A nor'easter is a storm that strikes the New England coast from the Northeast, bringing high winds and rain. It is particularly feared by sailors because it causes rough, dangerous seas.

What is a chinook?

A chinook is a warm wind that blows down the eastern slopes of the Rocky Mountains, especially in the spring. The chinook gains speed and generates warmth as it heads down the slopes. It can cause the temperature to rise as much as 50 degrees in a few hours, causing the most sudden change of weather known. It also can cause snow to melt suddenly and flood the surrounding areas.

In Wyoming and the Dakotas, chinooks can change the temperature so quickly that houses and other buildings "groan" as they expand in the sudden warmth.

What are the Santa Anas?

The Santa Anas are winds that come off the deserts of southern California, causing intense heat, dryness, and clear blue skies in cities along the coast. The winds along the California coast normally come from the Pacific Ocean, bringing moist, cool air. But when the Santa Anas blow, temperatures can go up to 100 degrees. These desert winds dry out trees and shrubs and cause serious danger from forest fires.

5

Plants and Animals

What kinds of plant life are there in the United States?

When the first settlers arrived, they were amazed to see the huge forests. They came to believe that the forests were endless. In the South, they found many trees and flowering plants that were new to them. These trees and plants would grow only in warm climates. Then, when the settlers reached the Midwest, they were surprised to find a vast "sea" of grasses on the prairies and plains. Finally, in the mountains of the west, they discovered huge forests of evergreen trees, including some of the largest and oldest living things in the world.

What is the largest tree in the United States?

The largest tree is a giant sequoia in Sequoia National Park in California. It is named the General Sherman in honor of a Civil War general. This giant evergreen tree has a trunk 36 feet thick, and it stands more than 270 feet tall. No other living thing is as large as the General Sherman. It is probably more than three thousand years old.

Is the General Sherman the tallest tree?

No. In northern California, about 300 miles from the General Sherman, there are groves of great redwood trees. These trees are much more slender than the giant sequoias, but they grow even taller. Some are more than 360 feet tall—the height of a thirty-story building.

The redwoods, too, can live many hundreds of years. Their wood is strong and has chemicals that keep insects and birds away. Some redwoods are cut down and their lumber is used as facing on houses and other buildings.

What is the oldest tree in the United States?

The sequoias live longer than almost any other living thing. But another kind of evergreen called the bristlecone pine lives even longer. The oldest known bristlecone pine also lives in California, about 100 miles from the General Sherman. It is called Methuselah, after the oldest man mentioned in the Bible. Scientists have determined that it is nearly 4,700 years old. This means that it began life in about 2700 B.C., around the time the ancient Egyptians were building the first pyramids.

Bristlecone pines are not nearly as large or as tall as the sequoias and redwoods. They live in near-desert lands and may look more like shrubs than trees. But they can live through heat, lack of water, and many other dangers. They are thought to be the oldest living things on earth.

What is a buckeye?

A buckeye is a kind of horse chestnut tree that settlers found growing in the Ohio River Valley. The large brown nut of the tree was called a buckeye because it reminded settlers of the eye of a deer (a male deer is a buck). The buckeye is the state tree of Ohio, which is known as the Buckeye State.

What is your state tree?

The following list shows all the states in alphabetical order and their state trees. See if you can find yours.

STATE TREES

State	Tree	State	Tree
Alabama	Southern pine	Montana	Ponderosa pine
Alaska	Sitka spruce	Nebraska	Cottonwood
Arizona	Paloverde	Nevada	Single-leaf piñon
Arkansas	Pine	New Hampshire	White birch
California	California redwood	New Jersey	Red oak
Colorado	Colorado blue spruce	New Mexico	Piñon
Connecticut	White oak	New York	Sugar maple
Delaware	American holly	North Carolina	Pine
Dist. Columbia	Scarlet oak	North Dakota	American elm
Florida	Sabal palmetto palm	Ohio	Buckeye
Georgia	Live oak	Oklahoma	Redbud
Hawaii	Candlenut	Oregon	Douglas fir
Idaho	White pine	Pennsylvania	Hemlock
Illinois	White oak	Rhode Island	Red maple
Indiana	Tulip poplar	South Carolina	Palmetto
Iowa	Oak	South Dakota	Black hills spruce
Kansas	Cottonwood	Tennessee	Tulip poplar
Kentucky	Kentucky coffee tree	Texas	Pecan
Louisiana	Cypress	Utah	Blue spruce
Maine	Eastern white pine	Vermont	Sugar maple
Maryland	White oak	Virginia	Dogwood
Massachusetts	American elm	Washington	Western hemlock
Michigan	White pine	West Virginia	Sugar maple
Minnesota	Red pine	Wisconsin	Sugar maple
Mississippi	Magnolia	Wyoming	Cottonwood
Missouri	Dogwood		

What is the most popular state tree?

The most popular state tree is the pine. Eight states have named some tree in the pine family as their state tree. Five of them are states along the northern border of the United States: Maine, Michigan, Minnesota, Montana, and Idaho. But pines also grow in the South; the other states that honor the pine are North Carolina, Alabama, and Arkansas. Many other states have spruce or fir trees (relatives of the pine) as their state tree.

The most popular broad-leafed trees are the oak (six states) and the maple (five states).

What state is called the Sunflower State?

Kansas. The huge, cheerful sunflowers grow wild in the plains states, and the sunflower is the state flower of Kansas.

Do all states have a state flower?

Yes and no. The "flower" of Maine is the cone and tassel of the pine tree. The state flower of New Mexico is the blossom of the yucca tree. Several other states have named the blossoms of fruit trees. Most states, however, have named a more common flower. Four states and the District of Columbia have picked some kind of rose.

What is the national bird of the United States?

The national bird is the bald eagle. Benjamin Franklin believed that the bald eagle was too cruel to be the national bird. He suggested the turkey instead. But others complained that the turkey was not very smart and would not be a good symbol for a strong, independent country.

The bald eagle is not bald at all; the white feathers on its head make it appear to be bald. It is a bird of prey that catches and kills small animals for food. Hundreds of thousands of bald eagles were shot or trapped before 1900, and today they are an endangered species. It is against the law to kill a bald eagle.

Where did the turkey come from?

The turkey is a fowl that was discovered in America. When the first explorers arrived, turkeys were living wild from Maine to Mexico. The Indians in Mexico had domesticated one kind of turkey and raised it for food.

Early settlers in the American colonies hunted wild turkeys, and they became the traditional food at feasts and celebrations. Today many people eat turkey, especially at Thanksgiving. The turkeys we eat today are different from the wild turkeys, though. The wild turkeys had tough, stringy meat and a very strong taste. The settlers roasted turkey much as we do—but first they boiled it for several hours to make it a little more tender.

What landlocked state has the sea gull as its state bird?

Utah. When the first Mormon settlers reached the state in 1847, they knew they would need crops to eat by the next summer. When they were just ready to harvest their first big crop, a swarm of grasshoppers appeared and began to eat the grain. It seemed that all the crops would be destroyed.

Just then, a flock of sea gulls appeared. The nearest sea is nearly 1,000 miles from that first Mormon settlement, but sea gulls lived around the Great Salt Lake nearby. The birds attacked the swarm of grasshoppers and saved the crops. The settlers were so grateful that they later built a monument to the sea gulls in Salt Lake City, and they made the sea gull the state bird of Utah.

What is your state flower?

The following table shows the states in alphabetical order with their state flowers. See if you can find your state's flower.

STATE FLOWERS

State	Flower	State	Flower
Alabama	Camellia	Mississippi	Magnolia
Alaska	Forget-me-not	Missouri	Hawthorn
Arizona	Saquaro cactus blossom	Montana	Bitterroot
		Nebraska	Goldenrod
Arkansas	Apple blossom	Nevada	Sagebrush
California	Golden poppy	New Hampshire	Purple lilac
Colorado	Rocky Mountain columbine	New Jersey	Purple violet
		New Mexico	Yucca blossom
Connecticut	Mountain laurel	New York	Rose
Delaware	Peach blossom	North Carolina	Dogwood
Dist. Columbia	American Beauty rose	North Dakota	Wild prairie rose
		Ohio	Scarlet carnation
Florida	Orange blossom	Oklahoma	Mistletoe
Georgia	Cherokee rose	Oregon	Oregon grape
Hawaii	Hibiscus	Pennsylvania	Mountain laurel
Idaho	Syringa	Rhode Island	Violet
Illinois	Native violet	South Carolina	Carolina jessamine
Indiana	Peony	South Dakota	
Iowa	Wild rose		Pasque flower
Kansas	Native sunflower	Tennessee	Iris
Kentucky	Goldenrod	Texas	Bluebonnet
Louisiana	Magnolia	Utah	Sego lily
Maine	Pine cone and tassel	Vermont	Red clover
		Virginia	Dogwood
Maryland	Black-eyed Susan	Washington	Western rhododendron
Massachusetts	Mayflower		
Michigan	Apple blossom	West Virginia	Big rhododendron
Minnesota	Pink-and-white lady's-slipper	Wisconsin	Wood violet
		Wyoming	Indian paintbrush

What is your state bird?

The following table shows the states in alphabetical order. See if you can find your state bird.

STATE BIRDS

State	Bird	State	Bird
Alabama	Yellowhammer	Missouri	Bluebird
Alaska	Willow ptarmigan	Montana	Western meadowlark
Arizona	Cactus wren		
Arkansas	Mockingbird	Nebraska	Western meadowlark
California	California Valley quail	Nevada	Mountain bluebird
Colorado	Lark bunting	New Hampshire	Purple Finch
Connecticut	American robin	New Jersey	Eastern goldfinch
Delaware	Blue hen chicken	New Mexico	Roadrunner
Dist. Columbia	Wood thrush	New York	Bluebird
Florida	Mockingbird	North Carolina	Cardinal
Georgia	Brown thrasher	North Dakota	Western meadowlark
Hawaii	Hawaiian goose		
Idaho	Mountain bluebird	Ohio	Cardinal
Illinois	Cardinal	Oklahoma	Scissor-tailed fly-catcher
Indiana	Cardinal		
Iowa	Eastern goldfinch	Oregon	Western meadowlark
Kansas	Western meadowlark	Pennsylvania	Ruffed grouse
Kentucky	Cardinal	Rhode Island	Rhode Island Red
Louisiana	Eastern brown pelican	South Carolina	Carolina wren
		South Dakota	Ring-necked pheasant
Maine	Chickadee		
Maryland	Baltimore oriole	Tennessee	Mockingbird
Massachusetts	Chickadee	Texas	Mockingbird
Michigan	Robin	Utah	Sea gull
Minnesota	Common loon	Vermont	Hermit thrush
Mississippi	Mockingbird	Virginia	Cardinal
		Washington	Willow goldfinch
		West Virginia	Cardinal
		Wisconsin	Robin
		Wyoming	Meadowlark

What state has a chicken named after it?

Rhode Island. The Rhode Island Red is a variety of chicken developed in the state and is the state bird. There is also a Rhode Island White chicken.

What are the most popular state birds?

The most popular of all is the cardinal, a brilliant red bird with a high tuft of feathers on its head. Seven states from Virginia to Illinois claim the cardinal. The second most popular is the meadowlark, which is claimed by six states from Kansas in the Midwest to Oregon on the Pacific Coast. The most popular bird in the South is the mockingbird, which is the state bird in five southern states.

What American is always connected with birds?

John James Audubon was born in Haiti and grew up in France. But he came to America as a young man in 1803 and devoted much of his life to studying and making paintings of American birds. His huge work, *Birds of America,* was finished in 1838 and had 435 full color paintings of birds. Later he studied other warm-blooded animals.

The National Audubon Society, founded in 1905, more than fifty years after Audubon died, is devoted to preserving birds and other wild animals. It operates bird sanctuaries and has many educational programs for both children and adults.

Did all the birds we know today always live here?

No. Some kinds of birds were brought to the United States from other parts of the world. In 1890 an Englishman brought several new kinds of birds to the United States and let them go free in Central Park in the middle of New York City. He thought it would be good for the United States to have birds that had only lived in Europe.

Some of the birds he let go were starlings. These birds multiplied very quickly here because they had few natural enemies, and in some parts of the United States they drove out other kinds of birds and became serious pests. All of the millions of starlings in the United States today are relatives of about sixty starlings released in 1890 and 1891.

What kind of animals are there in the United States?

Early settlers and explorers from Europe found many animals that were already familiar to them. But they also discovered many that seemed strange. They gave these "new" American animals new names, and some became great favorites.

Is a prairie dog really a dog?

No. The prairie dog is a member of the squirrel family. Early settlers discovered these creatures living in underground burrows in the plains and prairies of the Midwest. They live in large "prairie dog towns" and eat grasses and roots. The settlers called them prairie dogs because when they were in danger they warned others in the colony by making a shrill barking noise.

Farmers consider the prairie dog a pest, and millions have been killed to keep them from eating grain and digging burrows in farmers' fields.

What is a gopher?

A gopher is another burrowing animal slightly smaller than a prairie dog. Gophers rarely come out of their burrows, which can sometimes be hundreds of feet long. They eat grain, buds, seeds, and small plants. Minnesota is known as the Gopher State. Early settlers found many gophers on its southern prairies.

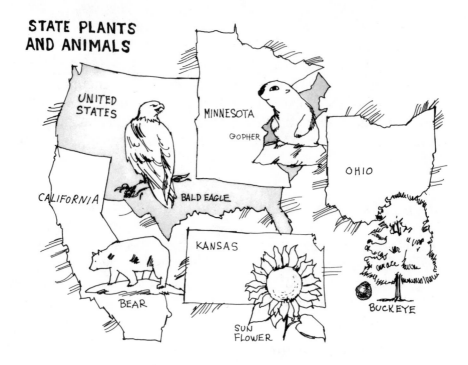

STATE PLANTS AND ANIMALS

UNITED STATES — BALD EAGLE

MINNESOTA — GOPHER

OHIO — BUCKEYE

CALIFORNIA — BEAR

KANSAS — SUN FLOWER

What is a badger?

A badger is another digging animal found on the prairies of the upper Midwest. It is a member of the weasel family, and it gets its name from the white marking (or badge) on its head and face. Wisconsin is known as the Badger State. Lead miners in the early days of the state worked in mines and sometimes lived in caves. They, too, were called badgers because they reminded people of the burrowing animal.

What is a wolverine?

The wolverine is a slightly larger relative of the badger. Wolverines once lived all over a large area of woodland in the northern United States and Canada. Early settlers considered them vicious because they seemed to kill other animals even when they were not hungry or in danger. Many thousands were trapped for their fur, and wolverines are now rare. Michigan is known as the Wolverine State because of the importance of the wolverine to trappers there in the early days of the state.

What animals were most useful to the early settlers?

The settlers found uses for many animals. They trapped beavers, wolverines, and other animals for their fur. They shot many small animals and birds for food. Sometimes an animal would help them by destroying insects or other pests.

When railroads were being built across the Great Plains, hunters discovered the huge herds of American bison, usually called buffalo. The Indians had hunted the buffalo for centuries. They used the meat for food and the hides for clothing and shelter. But the white hunters, with their powerful rifles, killed off nearly all of the buffalo in a few short years. Today there are only a handful of the huge creatures left, and they are protected in special preserves.

Which animals most frightened the settlers?

Probably the most terrifying creature was the bear. Different kinds of bears lived in the forests and mountains from New England to California. People did not always realize that most bears are shy and will fight only if they are cornered. They are not great hunters, and most of their diet is made up of berries, nuts, and plants. If a bear is frightened, however, it can be very dangerous. There are many stories of hunters surprising a bear and having to climb trees to escape. Since many bears can also climb trees, even this was sometimes dangerous. Oddly enough, people admired the huge creatures even though they were afraid of them. The golden bear is on the state seal of California.

In the Great Plains and the other vast open spaces of the West, where bears were not common, the most frightening animal was the wolf and its smaller cousin, the coyote. These members of the dog family were often more troublesome than bears because they are meat eaters and would kill livestock. At night they prowled around isolated houses, and their howling could be heard for great distances. Most settlers believed that a wolf would hunt and kill a person, even though there were few proven cases of this.

What is the strangest American animal?

Early settlers in Louisiana and other parts of the South discovered a creature they called the armadillo. The armadillo is a warm-blooded creature, but instead of having fur, it has a hard, bony plate of armor to protect it from its enemies. It lives in burrows in the ground and eats insects and other small creatures in the soil by licking them up with its long tongue.

What is the funniest American animal?

One animal almost as odd as the armadillo and more fun to watch is the opossum. The opossum is a distant relative of the kangaroo, but it looks more like a large rat with a long, hairless tail. When opossum babies are born, they are only about the size of the tip of a finger, and for the first two months they live safely in a pouch of skin on their mother's abdomen. After they come out of the pouch, they stay close to the mother and sometimes ride on her back or even clutch her tail with their own.

When an opossum is surprised by an enemy, it protects itself by lying down and "playing dead." After the enemy leaves, the opossum gets up and goes on its way. When we say that some person is "playing possum," we mean that he or she is only pretending to be hurt or defeated.

6

Creating the United States

Who were the first Americans?

The peoples we know as the American Indians. We believe that American Indians made their way to North America at least twenty thousand years ago. They came over a land bridge that connected Asia and North America between what is now Siberia in the Soviet Union and what is now the state of Alaska. By the time Columbus reached the Americas from Europe, there were probably a million Indians living in what is now the United States.

How did the Indians in America live?

There were many different tribes in America. Each tribe had its own language and customs. Indians in different regions lived very differently from each other. Sometimes neighboring tribes cooperated with each other. But often they fought with each other, too.

The Indian tribes that lived between the Atlantic Ocean and the Mississippi River are called Woodlands Indians. They were the first Indians the early American settlers met. They lived in villages and were farmers and hunters.

Were the Vikings the first Europeans to discover America?

Leif Eriksson was a Viking, one of a group of tribes who lived in Norway and other parts of Northern Europe. By the year A.D. 1000, the Vikings had already established colonies in Iceland and Greenland. Around that time, Leif Eriksson's tiny ship got blown off course and landed far to the west—probably along the coast of Canada. He is said to have called the new place Vinland. His visit is difficult to prove, but many people believe it happened. Not many people found out about Eriksson's voyage, and the Vikings were not able to establish a lasting settlement. So America remained a secret to most people in Europe.

Who was Christopher Columbus?

Christopher Columbus was an Italian sailor who explored for the king and queen of Spain. He was looking for a new sea route to the Indies, the islands in Asia where spices were grown. In 1492, almost five hundred years after Leif Eriksson, Columbus sailed westward from Spain and landed in the islands of the Caribbean Sea. He believed that he had sailed halfway around the world and had landed in the Indies.

Columbus made two more voyages to the islands, and his reports created great excitement in Europe. Soon other explorers were heading west to see what they could learn about the land Columbus told about. Gradually, people came to see that he had not reached the Indies, but the islands he discovered were called the West Indies, a name that is still used today.

Why wasn't the new land named after Columbus?

One of the explorers who followed Columbus was Amerigo Vespucci. Vespucci wrote a long report on his adventures, and in it he claimed that the lands across the Atlantic were a whole New World. His reports on his travels were widely read, and mapmakers began calling the new land America, after Vespucci's first name.

By the time people realized that Columbus was really the first explorer of the time to discover America, it was too late to change all those maps. Still, many places in the Americas are named after Columbus: the country of Colombia in South America, the District of Columbia in the United States, and many towns and cities named Columbia or Columbus.

After America was discovered, did people come to live here?

Not for many years. The first permanent settlement in what is now the United States was set up by the Spanish in 1565, almost seventy-five years after Columbus's first voyage. The Spanish called the settlement St. Augustine, and it is in what is now the state of Florida. For nearly fifty years, it was the only European settlement in the present-day United States.

What was the Lost Colony?

In 1585, twenty years after St. Augustine was founded, the English first tried to start a settlement in North America. A group of about one hundred sailed from England and landed on Roanoke Island, just off the coast of present-day North Carolina. Most of the settlers found life so hard that they sailed back to England less than a year later, leaving only fifteen people on the island. A new group of about one hundred settlers arrived in 1587. They found that all those who had stayed were dead.

When the next supply ship arrived from England in 1590, all the people on Roanoke Island had disappeared. There were a few clues, including the word "CROATOAN" carved on a tree. But no one ever found out what happened to those settlers. They are the Lost Colony.

Who was Virginia Dare?

A month after the second group of settlers arrived at Roanoke Island in 1587, a child was born to one of the women. The child was named Virginia Dare, and she was the first English child born in North America. News of her birth traveled back to England before Virginia and all the rest of the settlers disappeared.

What was the first lasting English colony?

In 1607, almost twenty years after the Lost Colony disappeared, new settlers arrived nearby. They founded the settlement of Jamestown, now in the state of Virginia. It was named for James I, who was then king of England.

In 1620, only a few years later, another group of Englishmen began a settlement 500 miles north of Jamestown. They called their colony Plymouth. Within a few years there were several other settlements nearby. The region came to be known as Massachusetts, and Plymouth is now in that state.

Did these early settlers meet the Indians?

Yes. In Jamestown the settlers met Indians in their very earliest days.

Were the Indians friendly?

Yes, at first. The settlers at Jamestown were met by the chief named Powhatan. He helped the settlers in their first difficult years. But later there were misunderstandings between the settlers and the English and Powhatan became an enemy of the settlers.

Who was Pocahontas?

Pocahontas was the daughter of the chief Powhatan. When she was twelve years old, Powhatan was an enemy of the settlers. He caught John Smith, the leader of the settlers, and was about to kill him when Pocahontas stopped her father and asked him to spare Smith's life.

Some years later, Pocahontas married one of the settlers, John Rolfe. She went to England with him, and was treated as an Indian princess. She died in England of smallpox before she could return home.

Were the Indians friendly to the Plymouth settlers?

Yes. In fact, they probably helped save the colony from starvation. One day an Indian named Samoset appeared in Plymouth and amazed the settlers by speaking to them in English. (He had learned English from English fishermen who sometimes stopped on the New England shores.) He soon returned with Squanto, an Indian who had actually traveled to England and Spain. Squanto showed the Pilgrims how to plant corn, and he acted as an interpreter when they worked out a treaty with the local chief, Massasoit.

Why didn't the Indians and the settlers stay friendly?

There were many reasons. Probably the most important is that they did not understand each other very well. For example, the settlers wanted to know who owned the land where they had settled. The Indians didn't understand. They said no one owned the land, because they believed the land was for all people. But when the settlers began to cut down the forests and put walls around the fields, the Indians were angry.

The Indians were also afraid of the settlers. Soon after the first settlers arrived, Indians began to die of measles and other European diseases. They died by the thousands, and some tribes were wiped out. The settlers also had guns, which seemed like terrible magic to people who had never seen one before.

The settlers were afraid of the Indians, too. They did not understand or respect the Indians' religion. They also thought that the Indians did not seem to work very hard, and they wanted to make more of the land than the Indians had.

Because of all these misunderstandings and fears, the settlers and the Indians were soon at war. The Indians sometimes won a battle, and they killed thousands of settlers. But the settlers had the stronger weapons and determination, and they almost always won in the end. The battles between settlers and Indians went on for nearly three hundred years (see Chapter 8).

Did the early settlers want to form their own country?

Not for a long time. They needed supplies from their mother country and they continued to think of themselves as English people. It was 150 years before the English colonists began a war for independence.

Did England claim all of the territory that became the United States?

No. They had many rivals because other countries of Europe claimed parts of North America.

What six countries once controlled parts of today's United States?

1. *Holland* controlled parts of New York and New Jersey from 1624 to 1664, when it gave them up to England.
2. *Britain* controlled the Atlantic Coast states, except Florida,

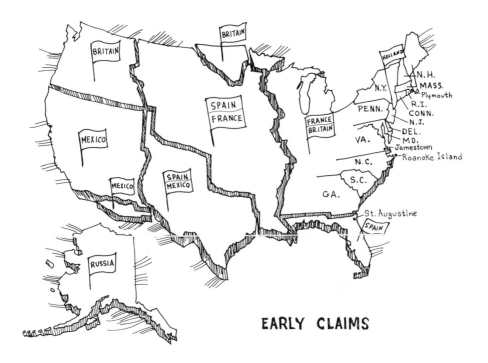

EARLY CLAIMS

from about 1660 until the end of the Revolutionary War in 1781. After the United States was formed, England still claimed parts of the Pacific Northwest as part of Canada.

3. *France* controlled eastern Canada until 1763 and claimed much of the land between the Ohio and the Mississippi rivers. Later, France still claimed a huge area west of the Mississippi River, running from New Orleans, north along the Mississippi and Missouri rivers.

4. *Spain* controlled Florida. In addition, its colony of Mexico stretched far north into the present-day United States, including all or part of Texas, Oklahoma, New Mexico, Colorado, Utah, Arizona, Nevada, and California.

5. *Mexico* became independent of Spain in 1821 and took over the lands Spain had claimed in the American Southwest.

6. *Russia*—now called the Soviet Union—began to make settlements in Alaska in the 1700s and claimed most of that state.

Were any parts of the United States once independent countries?

Yes. During the Revolutionary War, all thirteen colonies considered themselves independent. Many colonists thought that there would be thirteen countries when the war was over instead of just one.

Later, Texas became an independent country. In 1835 Texas was a part of Mexico, but most of the people living there were Americans. That year, the Texans declared their independence and fought a long, hard war against Mexico. Finally Mexico granted them their independence. Texas was a separate country until 1845, when it became a state in the United States.

The other territory that was once an independent nation was Hawaii. From the early 1800s until 1893 it was a kingdom ruled by native Hawaiians. From 1893 until 1898 it was a republic controlled by American landowners. In 1898 it became a territory of the United States and in 1959 it became a state.

What land did the United States have when it became a country?

At the end of the Revolutionary War in 1783 there were thirteen colonies, or states. They were the New England states of New Hampshire, Massachusetts, Rhode Island, and Connecticut; the Middle Atlantic states of New York, New Jersey, and Pennsylvania; and the southern states of Delaware, Maryland, Virginia, North Carolina, South Carolina, and Georgia.

The United States also controlled all the land as far west as the Mississippi River between the Great Lakes to the north and the Spanish territory of Florida to the south. This land included the territory that later became the five midwestern states of Ohio, Indiana, Illinois, Michigan, and Wisconsin; the later southern states of Tennessee and Kentucky; and parts of Alabama and Mississippi.

What was the Louisiana Purchase?

The Louisiana Purchase was the biggest sale of land in history. In 1803 President Thomas Jefferson learned that France was willing to sell its claims in the United States. These claims included much of the land between the Mississippi River and the Rocky Mountains—more than 800,000 square miles. Jefferson bought the land for about $15 million. It included all or part of fifteen states running from the Gulf of Mexico in Louisiana to the Canadian border of Montana. It nearly doubled the land area of the United States and opened huge new territories to settlement.

Who explored these new lands?

Even before President Jefferson had bought the land, he arranged to send an expedition to explore the Missouri River from St. Louis to its source. Jefferson was hoping that the expedition would be able to find a practical water route all the way to the Pacific Ocean.

The expedition was led by Meriwether Lewis and William Clark. They set out from St. Louis in May 1804 and returned more than two years later, in September 1806. The expedition spent its first winter in North Dakota. Then, after seven months of travel, they reached the Pacific Ocean in November 1805. The Lewis and Clark expedition was the greatest journey of exploration in American history.

Who was Sacajawea?

During the first winter in North Dakota, the Lewis and Clark Expedition hired a French-Canadian named Toussaint Charbonneau. Charbonneau was married to the Indian woman named Sacajawea, who travelled with the expedition all the way to the Pacific. Sacajawea was from the Shoshoni tribe that lived in the Rocky Mountains, and she served the expedition as an interpreter and as a guide through the rugged mountains. Her help in learning how to get through the Rockies and find a stream flowing to the Pacific saved the expedition from great danger.

How did the United States get territories from Spain?

Spain gave up its Florida territories in 1819, after U.S. troops invaded them. It lost the rest of its territories when Mexico declared its independence in 1821.

How did the United States get territories from Mexico?

Texas declared its independence from Mexico in 1835 and later became a state in the United States. In 1846 the United States declared war on Mexico over disputed territories between Texas and Mexico. At the end of that war in 1848, Mexico ceded (gave up) most of the land now in the southwestern states, including California, Nevada, Utah, and parts of Arizona and New Mexico, Colorado, and Wyoming.

What region was called Seward's Icebox?

Alaska. In 1867 William H. Seward was secretary of state. When he learned that the Russian government was eager to sell Alaska, he arranged to buy it. Others in the government said that he was crazy and that he had bought land worth nothing because it was so cold and so far away from the rest of the world. But the Congress approved of Seward's deal, and Alaska became a territory.

What is the newest land in the United States?

The Hawaiian Islands. The United States made Hawaii a possession in 1898.

How did the thirteen colonies become states?

The colonies had agreed to help one another out during the Revolutionary War. After the war they continued to cooperate. In 1787 they sent representatives to Philadelphia to a Constitutional Convention. The delegates wrote a Constitution that established the United States of America. The states had to approve, or ratify, the Constitution. The day a state approved the Constitution is the day we consider its birthday.

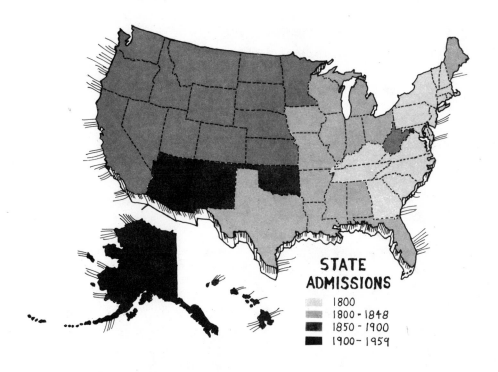

STATE
ADMISSIONS
1800
1800 - 1848
1850 - 1900
1900 - 1959

What was the first state?

The first state to ratify the Constitution was Delaware, on December 7, 1787. By June 1788 ten states had ratified it, and it took effect. Rhode Island was the last of the thirteen to approve, in May 1790.

How did a territory become a state?

The Constitution provided for the admission of new states by the Congress of the United States.

Why were some states "partnered"?

Before the Civil War, the northern and southern states were very suspicious of one another. The Congress could not get enough votes to admit a new state from one region without agreeing to admit one from the other region at about the same time. Thus a northern state like Indiana was admitted with a southern state like Mississippi. This agreement, or compromise, between the North and the South lasted until California was admitted by itself in 1850.

What two states joined the Union on the same day?

North Dakota and South Dakota, on November 2, 1889. Two more states, Montana and Washington, joined within nine days.

Have any states ever dropped out of the Union?

Yes. During the Civil War, the southern states from Virginia to Texas *seceded* from the United States to form a country called the Confederate States of America. This was one of the causes of the terrible Civil War. That war was fought between 1861 and 1865 between the North, which called itself the Union, and the South, which called itself the Confederacy. After the northern forces forced the South to surrender, the southern states were admitted back into the Union after they met certain requirements set by Congress.

When did your state join the United States?

You can find the answer on the following table.

STATES IN ORDER OF ADMISSION TO UNION

The Original Thirteen States		The Northern Expansion States	
1 Delaware	1787, Dec. 7	31 California	1850, Sept. 9
2 Pennsylvania	1787, Dec. 12	32 Minnesota	1858, May 11
3 New Jersey	1787, Dec. 18	33 Oregon	1859, Feb. 14
4 Connecticut	1788, Jan. 9	34 Kansas	1861, Jan. 29
5 Georgia	1788, Feb. 2	35 West Virginia	1863, June 20
6 Massachusetts	1788, Feb. 6	36 Nevada	1864, Oct. 31
7 Maryland	1788, Apr. 28	37 Nebraska	1867, Mar. 1
8 South Carolina	1788, May 23		
9 New Hampshire	1788, June 21	The Western Frontier States	
10 Virginia	1788, June 25	38 Colorado	1876, Aug. 1
11 New York	1788, July 26	39 North Dakota	1889, Nov. 2
12 North Carolina	1789, Nov. 21	40 South Dakota	1889, Nov. 2
13 Rhode Island	1790, May 29	41 Montana	1889, Nov. 8
		42 Washington	1889, Nov. 11
The Three Early States		43 Idaho	1890, July 3
14 Vermont	1791, Mar. 4	44 Wyoming	1890, July 10
15 Kentucky	1792, June 1	45 Utah	1896, Jan. 4
16 Tennessee	1796, June 1	46 Oklahoma	1907, Nov. 16
		47 New Mexico	1912, Jan. 6
The Partnered States		48 Arizona	1912, Feb. 14
17 Ohio	1803, Mar. 1		
18 Louisiana	1812, Apr. 30	The Disconnected States	
		49 Alaska	1959, Jan. 3
19 Indiana	1816, Dec. 11	50 Hawaii	1959, Aug. 21
20 Mississippi	1817, Dec. 10		
21 Illinois	1818, Dec. 3		
22 Alabama	1819, Dec. 14		
23 Maine	1820, Mar. 15		
24 Missouri	1821, Aug. 10		
25 Arkansas	1836, June 15		
26 Michigan	1837, Jan. 26		
27 Florida	1845, Mar. 3		
28 Texas	1845, Dec. 29		
29 Iowa	1846, Dec. 28		
30 Wisconsin	1848, May 29		

What are the two newest states?

Alaska and Hawaii. Both were admitted to the union in 1959. They are the only two states that have no border with any other state.

Will there be more states in the future?

It is possible. Some residents of Puerto Rico are in favor of statehood. But the United States has no other territories that are close to the U.S. mainland or big enough to become states. The only other way states might enter the Union is if an existing state would agree to break in half. Although people in northern California and in the region around New York City have talked about withdrawing from their states and becoming new states, it seems unlikely that this will ever happen.

7

Settlement and Immigration

Where did the early Americans come from?

The very earliest settlers came from England as we have already learned. But very soon afterward, they began coming from other countries as well. The Dutch and the Swedes had their own colonies for a few years, and even after these colonies were given up to England, many Dutch and Swedes stayed in America anyway. Soon thousands were coming from Scotland and Ireland, from France and Germany, and from many other countries as well.

Why did they leave their old homes and come to America?

There were many reasons. Some of the early settlers hoped to make a lot of money in the new country. Others just wanted some land and a chance to succeed; land was very hard to get in the crowded countries of Europe. Others came because they were being persecuted in their own country for their religious or political beliefs. They hoped to live in freedom in America. Still other early settlers came to make a new start because they had committed some crime in their own country.

How did they get to America?

The trip to America was a dangerous one—a long ocean voyage on a very small wooden sailing ship. Some of these ships were lost in storms, and on many others passengers caught diseases such as smallpox or cholera and died before reaching America. A person had to be brave or desperate to agree to come to America.

Where did the early immigrants settle?

The only part of the United States that was known to the earliest settlers was the Atlantic Coast. Nearly all the early settlements were within 50 miles of the sea. A few others were farther inland on major rivers.

Beginning in the 1700s the Spanish began new settlements along the Pacific Coast, establishing missions to bring Christianity to the Indians. But none of these missions had more than a handful of settlers from Europe.

Why did people begin to move West?

As the towns along the coast began to grow, a few especially adventurous men and women became curious about the land to the west. Their reasons for leaving the settlements and becoming pioneers were like their parents' reasons for leaving the countries of Europe: they hoped to make money; they wanted more land; they wanted a new start. Some went west when they were persecuted or handicapped because of their religious practices or political beliefs.

How did people get to the West?

At first they just followed the rivers upstream from the Atlantic. Some pushed on overland to discover new territory. The forests were full of fur-bearing animals, and so many early pioneers became trappers and hunters.

But soon they ran into the Appalachian Mountains. Today the Appalachians don't seem like much of a barrier. But to the early settlers—who were without roads or railroads and had no machinery to build highways, long bridges, or tunnels—the Appalachians seemed both impossible and frightening. No one knew for sure what was on the other side. They believed there were Indians and dangerous animals. In winter, the mountains received more cold and snow than the coastal lands. For many years, the Appalachians were the border of settlements in America.

What is a pass?

A pass is an easy way through a range of mountains. In the 1700s, hunters and trappers discovered that the land west of the Appalachians was promising farming country. If only people could get to it, it might be a great new area to live in. Explorers began to seek a way through or around the mountains that new settlers could take.

What was Cumberland Gap?

Cumberland Gap is a natural pass through the Appalachians. It runs through the Cumberland Mountains from western Virginia into Kentucky and Tennessee. The Gap was discovered around 1750, but was not widely known or used for many years. Then in 1775 Daniel Boone, the famous explorer and guide, blazed a "road" through the Gap. This Wilderness Road was the way most of the early settlers of Kentucky and Tennessee crossed the mountains. More than 200,000 people passed through Cumberland Gap before 1800. Later, railroads and highways passed through the Gap as well. Today the region is a National Historical Monument.

Did the settlers find other ways through the Appalachians?

Yes. Gradually other passes were found. In the early 1800s, the federal government helped build a major road through the Appalachians and into the heart of the Midwest. This route, which came to be known as the National Road, ran from Cumberland in western Maryland to Vandalia in southern Illinois. Parts of that early road are followed today by Interstate Highway 70, which runs from Baltimore to St. Louis and on across the Rocky Mountains.

Did everyone have to travel overland?

Yes, until 1825. By then the state of New York offered a water route to the West that actually went *around* the Appalachians rather than through them. It was the Erie Canal, which connected the Hudson River and the Atlantic Ocean with the Great Lakes. Travelers could sail up the Hudson River from New York City to Albany, New York; use the Erie Canal barges from Albany to Buffalo; then take a Great Lakes steamboat to Cleveland, Detroit, or even Chicago. The canal barges also carried freight, making it possible for farmers in the Midwest to ship their crops to the cities in the Northeast.

The Erie Canal helped make New York the most heavily populated state in the Northeast, and it made New York City the most important port along the Atlantic Ocean.

What is a trail?

In the 1840s thousands of people every week moved into the midwestern states, but a few daring people wanted to go even farther west. The Great Plains were still Indian territory, and the vast flatlands offered almost no protection to travelers. At the far end of the plains were the Rocky Mountains, which were twice as high and twice as rugged as the Appalachians. Beyond the Rockies were vast deserts and then more mountains. Altogether, between the Missouri River, where the frontier began, and the Pacific Ocean, there were more than 1,500 miles of wilderness.

The adventurous men and women who dared to cross this new wilderness needed more than a pass through the mountains. They needed a trail through the great open spaces of the West. They began to meet each spring at Independence, Missouri, to start the great trip to the West.

Where did the Oregon Trail run?

The Oregon Trail began in Independence, Missouri, and carried a traveler to Portland, in the beautiful Willamette valley of Oregon. It went overland to Kearney, Nebraska, then followed the Platte and North Platte Rivers through the high plains and into the Rocky Mountains. It used South Pass, the easiest pass through the Rockies, in western Wyoming, then turned northward into Idaho. From there it followed the course of the Snake and Columbia rivers to the Oregon Territory, ending at Portland.

The trail covered about 2,000 miles as it twisted and turned with the rivers and mountain valleys. Caravans left Independence only in the spring because the trip took nearly six months, and the mountain passes were blocked by snow in the winter. The travelers suffered hunger, cold, and exhaustion on the trip, and many of them died before reaching Oregon.

What were the other western trails?

Two of the other trails followed the same path as the Oregon Trail for at least part of the way. The Mormon Trail, followed by the Mormon pioneers who settled in Utah, went through Iowa and met the Oregon Trail at Fort Kearney, Nebraska. In western Wyoming, the Mormon Trail turned south toward the Great Salt Lake.

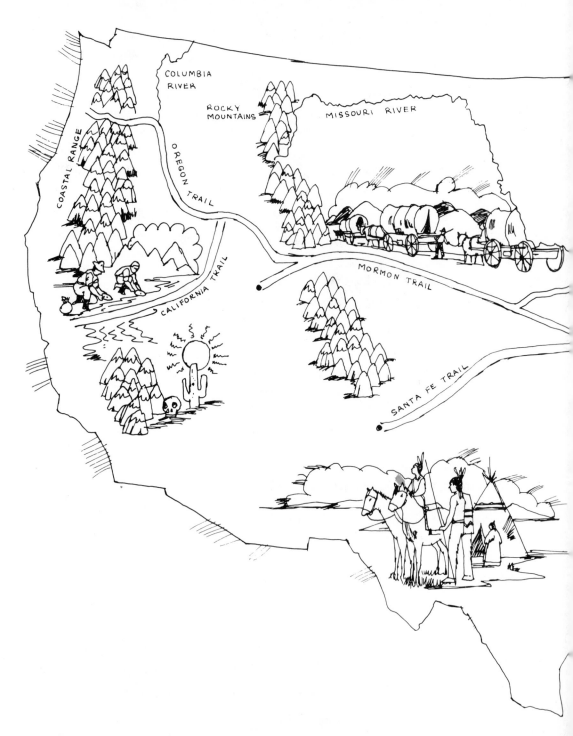

LAKE SUPERIOR

LAKE HURON

LAKE MICHIGAN

LAKE ONTARIO

LAKE ERIE

ERIE CANAL

HUDSON RIVER

NATIONAL ROAD

OHIO RIVER

WILDERNESS ROAD

CUMBERLAND GAP

APPALACHIAN MOUNTAINS

MISSISSIPPI RIVER

PASSES AND TRAILS

In 1849 thousands of excited travelers headed for California to share in the Gold Rush. Some of them went by sea, but many struck out overland. They followed the Oregon Trail as far as the Snake River in Idaho, then turned south and followed the Humboldt River through Nevada. Before reaching the gold fields of California, they had to cross the steep, rugged Sierra Nevada mountains. The trip to California was even more dangerous and tiring than the trip to Oregon.

Interstate Highway 80 now follows parts of the Oregon, Mormon, and California trails. The highway divides in Echo, Utah. From there, I-80 North goes northwest to Oregon, and I-80 South goes west to California.

One other great trail also began in Independence. It was called the Santa Fe Trail and ran clearly 800 miles to Santa Fe, New Mexico. It was an important connection between the early United States and the southwestern region held by Mexico until 1848. After 1848, it, too, carried pioneer settlers into new country. Its route was later followed by the Santa Fe Railroad.

What happened to the Indians?

Whenever settlers moved west, they pushed the Indians along ahead of them. The U.S. government often promised the Indians that they could have a part of the country forever. But then settlers wanted the land, and the Indians were forced to move again.

Many tribes did not give up easily, however. The tribes on the Great Plains had horses, and they became brave warriors. When they attacked a wagon train on the trail, the wagons would pull up in a circle for protection and try to hold off the fierce Indian bands. Indians also attacked small settlements, burning the buildings and killing the people.

Between 1840 and 1880, there were small battles between settlers and Indians almost every month. The U.S. Army set up forts along the frontiers and helped to protect the settlers.

What event ended the days of the wagon trains?

The coming of the railroad. In 1862 the U.S. Government offered the railroad companies huge rewards to build their rails from coast to coast. In the next few years, one company began to lay track eastward from Sacramento, California, and another company began to lay track west from Omaha, Nebraska. Only seven years later, in May 1869, the two tracks met in the mountains of northern Utah. After 1869 people could travel from Omaha to California in days rather than months.

Did new immigrants to the United States settle in any pattern?

Yes. People who arrived from other countries could settle anywhere in the United States. But many of them settled near others from their old homeland. Even today, there are neighborhoods and small towns that are mostly Irish, or Swedish, or Jewish or Italian.

If you had been an immigrant from Great Britain, where would you have settled?

Several different kinds of settlers came from Great Britain. The earliest settlers, including those who first arrived in Virginia and Massachusetts, were English. Many of the children and grandchildren of the original English settlers moved west, and they scattered throughout the country as they became Americans.

Later, many more immigrants came from other parts of Great Britain: Wales, Scotland, and Ireland. (Ireland was a part of Great Britain until 1919, when it became an independent country. Northern Ireland is still a part of Great Britain.) Perhaps the largest number were those who came to be known as Scotch-Irish. They were Protestant Scots who lived for a time in Northern Ireland, then came to America. They settled widely through the southern

United States, especially in western Virginia, western North Carolina, Kentucky, and Tennessee. Many American folk songs can be traced to songs these Scotch-Irish settlers brought with them.

If you had been a Dutch immigrant, where would you have settled?

The earliest Dutch settlers came to the land known as New Netherland—the parts of New York State that lie on Long Island and along the Hudson River. The Dutch gave up their colony to the English in 1664, but many continued to live in the region. Later settlers from Holland set up communities in western Michigan, and the town of Holland, Michigan, still has an annual tulip festival that celebrates its Dutch heritage.

If you had been a German immigrant, where would you have settled?

Germany contributed more immigrants to the United States after 1820 than any other country in the world. At first large numbers settled in Pennsylvania. The people known today as the Pennsylvania Dutch are descendants of German settlers, and many thousands of them still speak a dialect of the German language even though they have been in America for more than a hundred years.

More recent settlers from Germany clustered in parts of the Midwest. Such cities as Cincinnati, Ohio; St. Louis, Missouri; and Milwaukee, Wisconsin, still have large numbers of residents of German parentage. Many smaller towns in the Midwest also grew from German settlements. There were many towns with German names in the United States until World War I (1917–1918). Then, because Germany was an enemy of the United States, the names of many such towns were changed to non-German names.

If you had been a French immigrant, where would you have settled?

France sent many fewer immigrants to the United States than Germany or Great Britain did. Most French immigrants to North America came to Quebec in eastern Canada. There were early French settlers in Maine, Louisiana, and along the Mississippi River north to St. Louis. The Cajuns who live in Louisiana are descendants of the Acadians—French settlers from the Canadian province of Nova Scotia who were driven out by the English. Today there are also many French-speaking Americans in northern Maine, New Hampshire, and Vermont.

If you had been an Irish immigrant, where would you have settled?

A great wave of settlers from Ireland came to the United States in the 1840s. A great famine in Ireland forced many thousands to leave Ireland or starve to death. These Irish immigrants settled mostly in the large cities of the Northeast. Many other Americans considered the Irish ignorant and disliked their religious beliefs. Gradually, the children and grandchildren of the Irish immigrants gained political power in their cities and towns. The first Roman Catholic to be elected President was of Irish descent and came from Massachusetts. His name was John F. Kennedy, and he was elected in 1960.

If you had been a Scandinavian immigrant, where would you have settled?

Scandinavians—people from Norway, Denmark, and Sweden—also came to the United States to escape famine and poverty. The largest number arrived between 1860 and 1880. Some settled in large towns in the Northeast, but most of them traveled to the

Midwest, settling in Illinois, Iowa, Minnesota, Nebraska, and the Dakotas.

If you had been a Jewish immigrant, where would you have settled?

Since about 1890 several million Jewish immigrants have entered the United States seeking to avoid persecution in their old homes. Most of them came from parts of present-day Poland, the Soviet Union, Germany, and Austria. Many of them settled in New York City, which soon had the largest Jewish community in the world. Others settled in other large cities in the Northeast, Midwest, and West.

PLAINS

If you had been an Italian immigrant, where would you have settled?

The largest number of Italian immigrants came to the United States after 1900. They, too, settled in large cities, especially in the Northeast.

If you had been a Polish immigrant, where would you have settled?

Polish immigrants also came after 1900, and they settled in towns and cities in the Northeast and Midwest. Today the Chicago metropolitan area has the largest population of Polish descent.

PRAIRIE

If you had been black, where would you have settled?

Most black people did not come to America as immigrants, but as slaves. They were carried here in huge numbers between 1750 and 1815 and sold as property. Most of them were owned by landholders in the South, where slavery was important to the growing of cotton and other cash crops. Slavery was abolished in the southern states at the end of the Civil War in 1865, but most black people were too poor to move from that region of the country.

Beginning in about 1920, however, millions of blacks moved to the upper Midwest and the Northeast, seeking better jobs and living conditions. Today they make up the majority of the population in some northern industrial cities such as Detroit, but slightly more than half of all American blacks still live in the southern states.

If you had been a Puerto Rican, Cuban or Dominican immigrant, where would you have settled?

Immigrants from the Spanish-speaking islands of the Caribbean began coming to the United States only in the 1940s. Puerto Rico is a self-governing territory of the United States, and its citizens can enter this country without any limitation. Between 1940 and 1970 the Puerto Rican population of New York increased from a few thousand to more than a million. Many Americans of Puerto Rican descent also live in Florida.

Many citizens of Cuba and the Dominican Republic came to the United States in the 1960s and 1970s because of political revolutions at home. Many of them settled in Florida and in major cities of the Northeast.

If you had been a Mexican immigrant, where would you have settled?

Some Americans of Mexican descent are not immigrants at all. They are descendants of Mexican people who lived in lands ceded by Mexico to the United States in the 1800s. Many thousands of others immigrated to the states of the Southwest in the 1900s. California and Texas have the largest populations of Mexican-Americans. Many others live in other southwestern states and as far north and east as Chicago.

If you had been a Japanese or Chinese immigrant, where would you have settled?

The largest populations of both Japanese- and Chinese-Americans are in California and Hawaii. There are also substantial numbers of both groups in some large cities.

What other countries have sent large numbers of immigrants to the United States?

Many immigrants also came to the United States from most of the smaller countries of Europe. In recent years, there have been many immigrants from countries in Central and South America and from such Asian countries as the Philippines, Korea, and Vietnam.

In addition, thousands of people have moved from Canada to the United States at various times. (Thousands of others have moved from the United States to Canada.)

8
Wars

Have any wars been fought inside the United States?

Yes. Several wars have been fought inside the United States. Here are the most important ones:

French and Indian War	1754–1763
American Revolution	1775–1781
War of 1812	1812–1815
Civil War	1861–1865

In addition to these major wars, there have been many other battles and skirmishes. Between 1620 and 1900, there were many battles between the settlers and Indians in many parts of the present-day United States. Texas fought a war for independence from Mexico in the 1830s. And there was even some fighting in the present-day United States during World War II (1941–1945).

What was the French and Indian War and where was it fought?

During the 1750s the British and French went to war in North America over their claims to much of eastern Canada and the lands between the Appalachian Mountains and the Mississippi River. The people of the British colonies in America fought with the British against the French. Major battles were fought at Fort Duquesne near the city of Pittsburgh and at several forts in northern New York State. The French took these forts early in the war, but later lost them to the British and the colonists. The decisive battle of the war was fought at Quebec City in Canada, and the French were forced to surrender. They lost most of their possessions in North America.

What was the American Revolution and where was it fought?

The American Revolution—sometimes called the War for American Independence or the Revolutionary War—was fought between 1775 and 1781, mostly in the American colonies from Massachusetts in the north to Georgia in the south. Troops from the colonies under General George Washington fought the British in a long series of battles.

Where are Lexington and Concord?

Lexington and Concord were two small villages outside Boston, Massachusetts. In April 1775 British troops in Boston learned that some Americans in these villages had secretly stored guns and ammunition to fight with. The British marched out toward Lexington and Concord to capture the guns. But the villagers had been warned that the British were coming, and they fired at the troops and drove them away. This was the first battle of the Revolution.

Who warned the villagers in Lexington and Concord?

They were warned by a courageous man from Boston named Paul Revere. He learned that the British were planning the attack and rode out of Boston in the middle of the night to warn the people.

What is so important about the year 1776?

During 1776, the second year of the American Revolution, the leaders of the colonies met in Philadelphia and agreed to issue a statement proclaiming that the American colonies were independent and would no longer be governed by Britain. Thomas Jefferson wrote the statement, and others made small changes in it. Finally, on July 4, the delegates from the colonies approved it. The statement was called the Declaration of Independence, and ever since then, July 4 has been celebrated as the birthday of the United States.

Where did the American leaders meet?

The signers of the Declaration met in the building now called Independence Hall in Philadelphia. The building is now a national historical monument, and visitors can still see the room where the meetings took place. Just outside of Independence Hall is the Liberty Bell, which the people rang—along with all the church bells in Philadelphia—on July 8, 1776, to celebrate the signing of the Declaration of Independence.

What happened in Valley Forge?

The British armies in America were strong, and the American troops retreated from them during 1776 and most of 1777. The Americans lost first New York and then Philadelphia. In the winter of 1777–1778, they made their winter camp in Valley Forge, Pennsylvania, about 20 miles west of Philadelphia. They suffered greatly there because the winter was cold and they did not have enough food, shelter, or clothing. George Washington, who commanded the troops, did use the winter for some training, however, and when the terrible winter at Valley Forge was over, the army was still together and still ready and willing to fight.

Valley Forge was the great testing place of the Revolution. If the soldiers and their leaders had given up then and gone home, Britain would have won the war, and the United States might not have become an independent country.

What happened to help the Americans and end the war?

Two big things helped end the war. The first was the success of the American army, made possible by the bravery of the soldiers. The British had a plan to cut the colonies in two by sending an army down from Canada and another up the Hudson River. The American troops won several small battles near the Hudson and finally surrounded a British army at Saratoga, New York. They forced the army to surrender and took about five thousand prisoners.

The success at Saratoga helped France decide to fight on the side of the American colonies and to declare war on Britain. The help from France was the second important thing that helped the colonies win the war.

Where is Yorktown and what happened there?

Yorktown was a fortified town in Virginia near Chesapeake Bay on a strip of land between two rivers. After several years of fighting in the southern states, British General Cornwallis marched his army into Yorktown, hoping to join up with the British navy there.

Instead, he found himself surrounded by American and French troops on land and by the French navy in Chesapeake Bay. He was forced to surrender the whole British army under his command on October 19, 1781. News of this great defeat caused the British leaders to give up fighting and begin peace negotiations with the Americans. After the Battle of Yorktown, the American colonies were really independent!

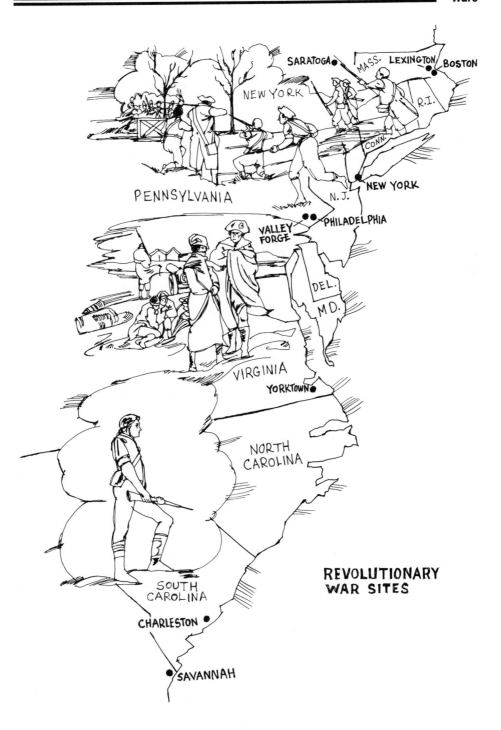

SARATOGA

MASS. LEXINGTON BOSTON

NEW YORK

R.I.

PENNSYLVANIA

CONN.

NEW YORK

N.J.

PHILADELPHIA

VALLEY FORGE

DEL.

MD.

VIRGINIA

YORKTOWN

NORTH CAROLINA

REVOLUTIONARY WAR SITES

SOUTH CAROLINA

CHARLESTON

SAVANNAH

Who said, "I regret that I have but one life to lose for my country"?

Nathan Hale was a young soldier who volunteered to become a spy for the Americans in New York in 1776 when the British held the city. Hale got the information he was sent for, but the British caught him and sentenced him to death. He made a speech that included this famous sentence just before the British hanged him. He was only twenty-one years old.

What was the War of 1812 and where was it fought?

The War of 1812 was the last war between Britain and its former colonies in North America. It was fought on land and on the lakes and seas of the eastern United States and Canada.

Why was the war fought?

The Americans were angry because Britain had been stopping its merchant ships on the seas, searching them, and carrying off some of their sailors. Also, some Americans hoped that the war might make Canada part of the United States. Some of the British hoped to gain land from the United States in the upper Midwest.

Who won the war?

When it was over, both sides claimed victory. But neither side accomplished what it had set out to do. Neither the United States nor Britain gained any territory, and the arguments about seizing merchant ships were not settled.

What damage did the United States suffer?

British troops in the Great Lakes region drove the Americans out of Detroit and burned part of the town. They also destroyed Buffalo, New York. The most serious and discouraging damage, however, occurred in Washington, the new U.S. capital. British troops sailed up the Potomac River, captured Washington, and burned the Capitol Building, the White House, and other public buildings.

What song came from the War of 1812?

Our national anthem. In 1814 Francis Scott Key and another American visited a British ship in Chesapeake Bay, hoping to gain the release of an American prisoner. The British agreed to the exchange, but insisted on holding all three men overnight while the British fleet bombarded Fort McHenry near Baltimore.

The Americans paced the deck all night, worried about the battle. They couldn't tell if the fort had survived the British attack. Finally, about dawn, through a break in the smoke and haze, Key saw the American flag still flying above the fort. He was inspired to write four verses of "The Star-Spangled Banner," with this familiar refrain:

> Oh, say, does that star-spangled banner yet wave
> O'er the land of the free and the home of the brave?

The verses were printed the very next day, and within a week they had been set to the tune we still use today. The words and the music became the official national anthem in 1931.

What was "the unnecessary battle"?

The War of 1812 was officially ended by the Treaty of Ghent (a city in Belgium), which was signed December 24, 1814. But there were

no radios, telephones, or telegraphs in 1814 to send the word to America that a peace treaty had been signed.

Two weeks later, on January 8, 1815, the British sent a force of eight thousand men to capture New Orleans from the Americans. The city was skillfully defended by Americans under the command of General Andrew Jackson. In the largest battle of the whole war, the Americans killed or wounded fifteen hundred British soldiers and reported only a few casualties themselves.

When news of the battle reached the rest of the country, it made Jackson a hero and helped elect him President years later. The battle was unnecessary, but it still had important results.

What was the Alamo and what happened there?

The Alamo was an old Spanish mission in San Antonio, Texas. In 1835, when the Texans rebelled against Mexico, the Mexicans sent an army under General Santa Anna to end the rebellion. When he arrived at San Antonio in February 1836 with five thousand men, the Texans took cover in the Alamo. There were fewer than two hundred of them.

On February 23 Santa Anna's army surrounded the mission and besieged it. After almost two weeks the Texans in the fort were running out of ammunition. On the morning of March 5 the Mexicans stormed the fort. When the battle was over, all but eight of the Texans were dead. Santa Anna had those eight put to death, too. Not one fighting man survived. Among those who died were two legendary frontier heroes, Davy Crockett and Jim Bowie.

The courage of the men at the Alamo rallied the people of Texas to fight for their independence. "Remember the Alamo!" they cried. The battle also gave Texas General Sam Houston time to gather a larger army. Only six weeks after the Alamo fell, Houston attacked and beat the Mexican army at San Jacinto. He captured Santa Anna and forced him to grant independence to Texas.

What was the Civil War and where was it fought?

The Civil War between the northern and southern states of the United States was the most destructive war in American history. It was fought between 1861 and 1865, and there were major battles in a dozen states, from Pennsylvania in the Northeast to Texas in the Southwest. More than half a million people died as a result of the war.

What were the causes of the Civil War?

For many years, the northern and southern states had been arguing with one another more and more often. One major disagreement between the two regions centered on slavery. The South used slaves as workers on large plantations; in the North many people believed that slavery was wrong and should be ended. There were many other disagreements: southerners believed that states should have more power than the national government, but northerners disagreed. The northern states were also growing much more rapidly than the South, and southern politicians saw that they would soon be outnumbered in the national government.

The final break between the North and South came with the election of Abraham Lincoln as President in 1860. He was not an acceptable President to southerners. In the early months of 1861 the southern states voted one by one to withdraw from the United States, and soon afterward they began to set up a new country, the Confederate States of America. Lincoln believed that the southern states could not legally leave the United States, and he promised to preserve the Union even if he had to go to war.

Which states fought on which side during the Civil War?

Eleven states joined the Confederate side. They were:

Virginia	Mississippi
North Carolina	Tennessee
South Carolina	Louisiana
Georgia	Arkansas
Florida	Texas
Alabama	

In these eighteen states slavery had already been outlawed, and they were all part of the Union:

Maine	Ohio
New Hampshire	Indiana
Vermont	Michigan
Massachusetts	Illinois
Rhode Island	Wisconsin
Connecticut	Iowa
New York	Minnesota
New Jersey	California
Pennsylvania	Oregon

In addition, there were four "border" states. These states had allowed slavery before the war, but they chose to remain with the Union:

Delaware	Kentucky
Maryland	Missouri

Finally, two new states were admitted to the Union just before or during the war. One was Kansas, which was admitted in January 1861, just as the southern states were seceding. The second was West Virginia, which was made up of the western counties of Virginia. The people in these counties wanted to stay in the Union when Virginia seceded, and so West Virginia became a state in the middle of the war.

What happened at Fort Sumter?

Fort Sumter was a small fort guarding the entrance to the harbor of Charleston, South Carolina. South Carolina had seceded from the United States, but U.S. troops still manned the fort. The government of the state would not allow the United States to bring in food or supplies to the soldiers at Fort Sumter, but the U.S. government decided to send supplies anyway. On April 12 soldiers of the new Confederate States fired on Fort Sumter, and two days later the Union soldiers in the fort surrendered. This began the Civil War.

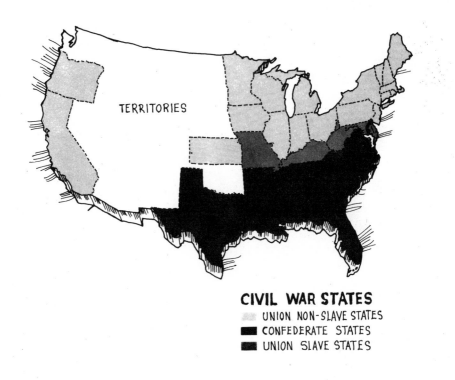

CIVIL WAR STATES
- UNION NON-SLAVE STATES
- CONFEDERATE STATES
- UNION SLAVE STATES

What were the main battlefields of the Civil War?

Union and Confederate troops fought for the land between Washington, D.C., the Union capital, and Richmond, Virginia, the Confederate capital, for almost all of the four years. Twice the Confederate armies tried to march north around Washington, bringing on major battles in Maryland and Pennsylvania.

A second series of major battles occurred in a belt of land that runs through the Confederate states from western Tennessee to Atlanta, Georgia.

A third series of battles took place on and near the Mississippi River between St. Louis, Missouri, and New Orleans, Louisiana.

What was the biggest battle of the Civil War?

The biggest battle was fought in July 1863 at Gettysburg, Pennsylvania. It was the only major battle of the war that was fought on the soil of a non–slave state. Robert E. Lee, the great Confederate general, had marched his men around the Union army and into Pennsylvania, hoping to discourage the Union. The Union army marched out of Washington, and the two sides met at the small crossroads town of Gettysburg. The fighting went on for three long days. In the end, the Union forces held the town, and the Confederate army was forced to retreat to its territory in Virginia. Nearly forty thousand men were killed or wounded in the three terrible days of fighting.

What was the Gettysburg Address?

In November 1863, five months after the Battle of Gettysburg, President Lincoln was invited to a ceremony dedicating part of the battlefield as a cemetery for the soldiers who died there. Another man, Edward Everett, was the main speaker that day, and he spoke for more than two hours. Then Lincoln stood up to make his brief remarks. The speech, which lasted only two or three minutes, has become the most famous ever delivered by an American. Lincoln outlined the cause he believed the Union was fighting for, ending with these famous words:

> It is rather for us to be here dedicated to the great task remaining before us—that from these honored dead we take increased devotion to that cause for which they gave the last full measure of devotion; that we here highly resolve that these dead shall not have died in vain; that this nation, under God, shall have a new birth of freedom; and that government of the people, by the people, for the people, shall not perish from the earth.

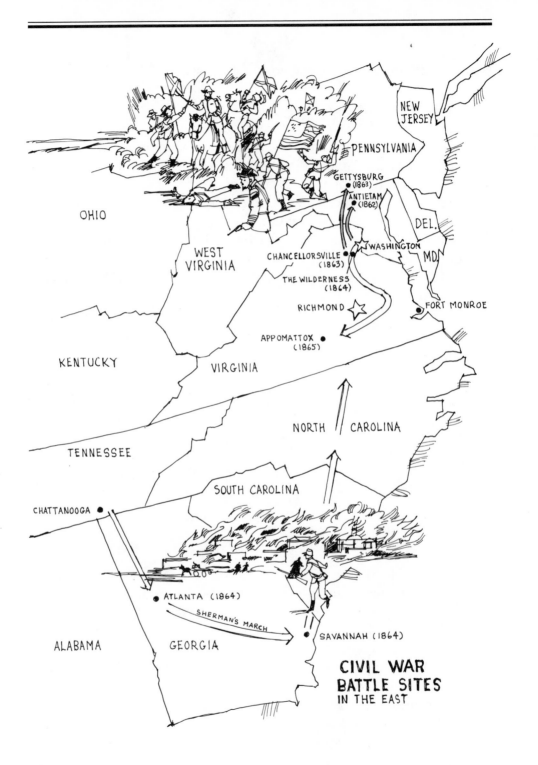

OHIO

NEW JERSEY

PENNSYLVANIA

GETTYSBURG
(1863)

ANTIETAM
(1862)

DEL.

WEST
VIRGINIA

CHANCELLORSVILLE
(1863)

WASHINGTON

MD.

THE WILDERNESS
(1864)

RICHMOND

FORT MONROE

APPOMATTOX
(1865)

KENTUCKY

VIRGINIA

NORTH   CAROLINA

TENNESSEE

SOUTH CAROLINA

CHATTANOOGA

ATLANTA (1864)

SHERMAN'S MARCH

SAVANNAH (1864)

ALABAMA   GEORGIA

CIVIL WAR
BATTLE SITES
IN THE EAST

What was Sherman's March to the Sea?

William Tecumseh Sherman was a Union general. He took command of the Union troops in Chattanooga, Tennessee, in 1864, and began a long series of battles aimed at capturing Atlanta. Atlanta fell to his army on September 2. The Confederate army, commanded by General John B. Hood, began to attack the railroad between Atlanta and Chattanooga, which brought food for the Union soldiers. He thought Sherman would have to come out and fight to keep the railroad open.

Instead, Sherman decided to give up his supply line and march in the other direction—from Atlanta to the sea at Savannah, Georgia. His sixty thousand soldiers caused terrible destruction and suffering along a path of 30 to 50 miles wide. Sherman's success made him a great hero in the North, but he is still remembered with terror and hatred in the South.

Where is Appomattox and what happened there?

The Union commander, General Ulysses S. Grant, had driven the Confederate armies back to Richmond, their capital, by July 1864. The Union armies dug trenches and waited for the Confederate cause to collapse. The people of Richmond had trouble getting enough food to eat, and there were not enough guns or ammunition for the soldiers, but the city was still too strong for the huge Union army to take.

Finally, in March 1865, the Confederacy began to collapse. Grant took the town of Petersburg, cutting off important railroad connections for Richmond. General Lee knew he would have to give up Richmond or see his army starve to death. The Confederates retreated to the west, but the Union armies followed close behind, cutting off any escape to the south and keeping supplies from the starving southerners.

On April 8 Lee sent a letter to General Grant asking for a meeting to discuss surrender. The next day they met at the small settlement of Appomattox Court House, Virginia, and agreed on terms for surrender. Within a few weeks other Confederate generals had surrendered, and the war was over.

What were the Indian Wars?

When the first settlers arrived from Europe in the early 1600s, there were more than a million Indians living in the territory that is now the forty-eight connected states. Gradually the settlers took the land away from the Indians. Sometimes the settlers bought the land or signed treaties for it, but often they took it by force. Small battles between Indians and settlers began early in the 1600s and continued for nearly three hundred years. The last bands of Apache warriors in the American Southwest were rounded up in about 1900.

Indians often attacked small settlements on the frontier and massacred people. At the same time, the settlers treated the Indians with great cruelty. The Indian Wars are a sad part of American history, both for the Indians and for the settlers.

What was Custer's Last Stand?

George Custer was an army officer who first gained fame in the Civil War. After the war, he was assigned to the Montana Territory where U.S. Army troops were rounding up the Sioux and Cheyenne Indians and bringing them to government reservations. The Indians didn't want to move to the reservations, and they fought the soldiers who tried to round them up.

In June 1876 Custer was ordered to take a regiment of 650 men to round up the people in an Indian village. He sighted the village on the banks of the Little Big Horn River in southern Montana and estimated that there were about 1,000 Indians in the village. It turned out that there were more than 3,000. He divided his men into three columns and ordered them to attack. Two of the columns

CUSTER'S LAST STAND

were defeated, but they managed to stay together until help arrived. But the column of 250 men commanded by Custer himself was wiped out; not one man remained alive.

Where is Wounded Knee and what happened there?

Wounded Knee was a U.S. Cavalry camp on Wounded Knee Creek in South Dakota. In 1890 the Ghost Dance movement broke out among the Sioux Indians. It was a religious movement seeking to recover the spirit of the times before the settlers. The army was afraid the movement would lead to more uprisings.

The army sent a detachment to round up the Indians who had left the reservation. They took about 350 of them to the cavalry camp at Wounded Knee. But when the soldiers tried to take the

Indians' guns, fighting broke out. In the next few minutes three hundred Indian men, women, and children were slaughtered by the soldiers. The army called the event a battle. But the Indians—and most historians—considered it a massacre.

Where are American Indians today?

For many years Indians were forced to live on reservations. Today there are still about 285 reservations, but Indians can choose whether or not to live on them. About half of them do and half don't.

In the 1970s many younger Indians began to demand that the federal and state governments make up for the many wrongs that had been done to Indians. In 1973 a group occupied the town of Wounded Knee, South Dakota, to call attention to their demands. Indians in many parts of the country are trying to recover the lands their ancestors lived on for thousands of years.

Have there been any other recent battles on American soil?

Yes. On December 7, 1941, Japanese planes attacked the huge U.S. Naval Base at Pearl Harbor in Hawaii. (In 1941 Hawaii was a territory of the United States, not a state.) The attack surprised the base on a Sunday morning, and hundreds of American servicemen were killed and injured. Part of the U.S. Pacific Fleet was destroyed.

The following day the United States declared war on Japan and Germany, entering World War II, which had been going on in Europe for more than two years.

Later, in 1942, the Japanese captured some of the islands in the Aleutian chain, part of the territory of Alaska. U.S. forces recaptured the islands in 1943.

These were the only two attacks on U.S. territory during World War II.

9
Government

How many Presidents has the United States had?

Ronald Reagan is the thirty-ninth man to serve as President. Sometimes he is called the fortieth President, however, because one President, Grover Cleveland, is sometimes counted twice. He served four years as President (1885–1889), was defeated when he ran for reelection, but then was elected to another term four years later (1893–1897). So some people count him as the twenty-second *and* the twenty-fourth President.

How long does a President serve?

A President is elected to a term of four years. The election takes place in November, and the President takes office early the following year. A President can be reelected for a second term, but he or she cannot be elected for more than two terms.

What are the requirements to be President?

The Constitution says that a President must be a "natural born citizen" of the United States, must have lived in this country for at least fourteen years, and must be at least thirty-five years old.

Could a woman be President?

Yes, but no woman has yet been elected.

What are the requirements to vote in a presidential election?

All citizens of the United States who are at least eighteen years old are qualified to vote in presidential and most other elections. The only exceptions are those who are convicted of certain serious crimes and those who are judged insane.

When the Constitution was first adopted, voting rights were confined to white men over the age of twenty-one. Some states made ownership of land or other property a requirement. Amendments to the Constitution have given voting rights to black men (1870), to women (1920), to those living in the District of Columbia, for President only (1961), and to those between eighteen and twenty years old (1971).

Which President served for the longest time?

The law that limits a President to two terms was passed in 1951. Before that, a President could be elected to any number of terms. Only one President, however, was ever elected to more than two terms. He was Franklin Delano Roosevelt, who was elected four times, in 1932, 1936, 1940, and 1944. Roosevelt took office on March 4, 1933. He died on April 12, 1945, only a few weeks into his fourth term. So he served a total of twelve years, one month and nine days. No other President has served more than eight years.

How many Presidents died while in office?

Eight of the first thirty-eight died while serving. Four died of illness and four were killed by assassins. They are:

William Henry Harrison,	died 1841,	illness
Zachary Taylor,	died 1850,	illness
Abraham Lincoln,	died 1865,	assassination
James Garfield,	died 1881,	assassination
William McKinley,	died 1901,	assassination
Warren Harding,	died 1923,	illness
Franklin Roosevelt,	died 1945,	illness
John F. Kennedy,	died 1963,	assassination

Who served the shortest time as President?

William Henry Harrison was the most unlucky President. At the ceremonies on the day he took office, March 4, 1841, he caught a cold, which later turned into pneumonia. He died April 4, 1841, after serving only thirty-two days.

One other President, James Garfield, served less than a year. He died of wounds caused by an assassin on September 20, 1881, six and a half months after taking office.

What happens when a President dies or resigns while in office?

The Vice-President, who was elected with the President, fills the office until the next election.

How many Vice-Presidents have become President in this way?

Nine. Five of these served as President without ever being elected to that office. The other four were later elected to a term of their own. They are Theodore Roosevelt (1901–09), Calvin Coolidge (1923–29), Harry Truman (1945–53), and Lyndon B. Johnson (1963–69).

Who was the youngest President?

Vice President Theodore Roosevelt became President on September 14, 1901, the day President McKinley died. He was six weeks short of his forty-third birthday. The youngest President to be elected was John F. Kennedy, who was forty-three years and about eight months old when he took office in 1961.

Who was the oldest President?

The oldest President at the time he took office was Ronald Reagan, who was three weeks short of his seventieth birthday when he became President on January 20, 1981. In May 1981 he also became the oldest man ever to serve as President.

Were any of the Presidents related to each other?

Yes. John Adams (1797–1801) and John Quincy Adams (1825–1829) were father and son. William Henry Harrison (1841) and Benjamin Harrison (1889–1893) were grandfather and grandson. Theodore Roosevelt (1901–1909) and Franklin Roosevelt (1933–1945) were distant cousins. Theodore was also the uncle of Franklin's wife Eleanor.

Two other Presidents had the same last name—Andrew Johnson and Lyndon Johnson—but they were not related.

WHO IS ON THE MONEY?

Were all the Presidents married?

Every President but one was married at some time in his life. The exception is James Buchanan, who served from 1857 to 1861.

Which President had the most children?

John Tyler (1841–1845) was the father of fourteen children. Seven of them were born to his first wife, who died while he was President. The other seven were born to his second wife, whom he married in a White House ceremony, after he left the presidency.

Did any Presidents have small children when they were in office?

Yes. When Theodore Roosevelt became President, he had five children ranging in age from seventeen to four. He once said of his oldest daughter Alice, "I can manage Alice or I can manage the country. I can't do both." Alice had a huge White House wedding in 1906 and died in 1980 at the age of ninety-six.

John Kennedy and his wife Jacqueline had a three-year-old daughter, Caroline, and a two-month-old son, John, Jr., when he took office in 1961. Jimmy Carter's daughter Amy was nine years old when her father was elected President in 1977.

Did any President have a physical handicap?

Yes. Franklin Roosevelt's legs were severely paralyzed by polio when he was a young man. He could not stand without heavy braces on his legs and could not walk without help. His family wanted him to give up politics after his illness, but he was elected governor of New York a few years later and then elected to four terms as President.

Who was the biggest President?

William Howard Taft (1909–1913) weighed more than 300 pounds. He had a special large bathtub installed in the White House. But he was a graceful dancer, according to writers of the time, and he took good care of his health. After leaving the presidency, he became a law professor, served in important government positions during World War I, and finally became Chief Justice of the Supreme Court (1921–1930).

Abraham Lincoln stood 6 feet 4 inches tall, and was the tallest of our Presidents. He seemed almost a giant to people in the 1860s.

What two Presidents died on the same day?

John Adams and Thomas Jefferson both died on July 4, 1826. It wasn't just any day, either: it was the fiftieth anniversary of the signing of the Declaration of Independence. Jefferson had written the Declaration, and Adams had helped revise it. Both men were determined to live to see that great anniversary. They were the last of the Founding Fathers.

What state is the birthplace of the most Presidents?

Virginia with eight. Four of the first five Presidents—Washington, Jefferson, Madison, and Monroe—came from Virginia. The other four were William Henry Harrison, John Tyler, Zachary Taylor, and Woodrow Wilson.

Ohio comes in a close second with seven Presidents. New York claims four native Presidents and Massachusetts three.

Only seventeen states have ever sent a native son to the presidency. The other thirty-three states are still waiting.

Which Presidents were military heroes?

Several Presidents were elected partly because of their military accomplishments. The first of these was George Washington, who had been the commander of the American armies in the American Revolution. Eight years after that war was over, Washington was elected our first President.

The next military hero was Andrew Jackson. He won the "unnecessary battle" of New Orleans against the British in the War of 1812 and later fought the Seminole Indians in the South. William Henry Harrison and Zachary Taylor also commanded troops against both the British and the Indians.

Ulysses S. Grant became the commanding general of the Union (Northern) forces during the Civil War. He was elected President three years after the war was over. Theodore Roosevelt was not a professional soldier, but he organized a cavalry unit called the Rough Riders and fought in Cuba in the Spanish-American War.

The most recent military hero was Dwight D. Eisenhower. During World War II, Eisenhower became the commander of Allied Forces in Europe and commanded the invasion of France in 1944. He was elected in 1952 and served two terms.

Two recent Presidents served in the Navy. John F. Kennedy commanded a PT boat during World War II. And Jimmy Carter was a graduate of the U.S. Naval Academy and served in the nuclear submarine program.

Who was the most famous and active President's wife?

The wives of several Presidents became very popular. But probably the most famous of all was Eleanor Roosevelt, the wife of Franklin Roosevelt. When her husband was President, Mrs. Roosevelt made many fact-finding trips for him, both in the United States and to other countries. After his death in 1945, she became a delegate to the first sessions of the United Nations in San Francisco. The next year she became chairman of the UN Human Right Commission. Mrs. Roosevelt also wrote a weekly column for many years and published several books.

Has any President ever been removed from office?

The Constitution provides a way—called impeachment—to remove a President from office if he or she is guilty of serious crimes. No President has ever been removed from office this way, but two came close.

Andrew Johnson (1865–1869) was charged with serious crimes by the House of Representatives and stood trial before the Senate. In order to remove him from office, two-thirds of the senators had to vote to convict. More than half of them voted to convict, but they were one vote short of the two-thirds majority. Johnson stayed in office, but he did not run for reelection.

Richard Nixon (1969–1974) was accused of serious crimes in 1974 by a committee of the House of Representatives, and it seemed certain that the full House of Representatives would vote to send him to trial. Before that could happen, however, Nixon resigned from the presidency on August 9, 1974. He was the first President ever to resign. A few weeks later, President Gerald Ford pardoned Nixon for any crimes he might have committed while in office.

How is the U. S. government organized?

There are three "branches" of the government. The executive branch, headed by the President, runs the day-to-day business of the government and sees that the laws are obeyed and carried out.

The legislative branch, or the Congress, makes the laws for the country.

The judicial branch, which includes the Supreme Court and other courts, helps decide what the Constitution and the laws passed by Congress mean and how they should be applied.

What is the Congress?

The Congress is a gathering of men and women who have been elected to represent a state or district. These representatives meet each year to make the laws and regulations that govern the country. There are two houses of Congress: the Senate and the House of Representatives. Most laws must be considered and passed by both the Senate and the House.

How does the Senate work?

There are two senators from every state, no matter how many people or how much land the state has. Since there are fifty states, there are one-hundred senators. The Senate considers laws and regulations—called bills—along with the House of Representatives. When both houses have passed the same bill, it is sent to the President to be signed. When the President signs the bill, it becomes a law.

The Senate also has some special jobs. When the President nominates someone for an important government job, the Senate must approve the nomination. The Senate must also approve all important treaties with other countries.

How long does a senator serve in the Senate?

A senator is elected by all the voters of a state and serves a six-year term. About a third of the places, or "seats," in the Senate come up for election every two years. The terms of senators from the same state never end in the same year.

What are the requirements to be a senator?

A senator must have been a citizen of the United States for at least nine years, must be at least thirty years old, and must live in the state he or she represents.

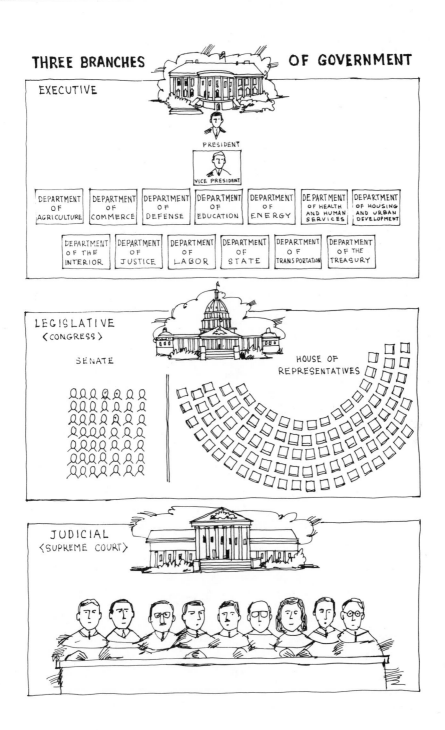

THREE BRANCHES OF GOVERNMENT

EXECUTIVE

PRESIDENT

VICE PRESIDENT

| DEPARTMENT OF AGRICULTURE | DEPARTMENT OF COMMERCE | DEPARTMENT OF DEFENSE | DEPARTMENT OF EDUCATION | DEPARTMENT OF ENERGY | DEPARTMENT OF HEALTH AND HUMAN SERVICES | DEPARTMENT OF HOUSING AND URBAN DEVELOPMENT |

| DEPARTMENT OF THE INTERIOR | DEPARTMENT OF JUSTICE | DEPARTMENT OF LABOR | DEPARTMENT OF STATE | DEPARTMENT OF TRANSPORTATION | DEPARTMENT OF THE TREASURY |

LEGISLATIVE
(CONGRESS)

SENATE

HOUSE OF REPRESENTATIVES

JUDICIAL
(SUPREME COURT)

Can a woman be a senator?

Yes. Hattie Caraway of Arkansas was the first woman elected to the Senate, winning election in 1932. Margaret Chase Smith of Maine served the longest of any woman, from 1949 until 1973.

Who runs the Senate's meetings?

The Vice-President of the United States. The Vice-President cannot vote in the Senate unless there is a tie. Then his or her vote can be used to break the tie. If the Vice-President cannot be at a meeting of the Senate, one of the senators is chosen to run the meeting.

How does the House of Representatives work?

There are 435 representatives or congresspersons. Each represents a *district* in a state with about the same number of people. States with many people have many districts. States with few people may have only one. For example, California, the state with the most people, has forty-five representatives. Alaska and five other states with the fewest people have only one representative.

Who decides how many representatives a state should have?

Since the populations of the states change, the government takes a *census* every ten years to determine how many people each state has and how many representatives it should have in the House. The last census was taken in 1980, and another will be taken in 1990. If a state grows faster than the other states, it will gain new representatives after a census. If it grows more slowly than the other states, it will lose representatives. For example, the fast-growing states of Florida, Texas, and California all gained new representatives after the 1980 census. New York, which lost population since the last census, lost representatives.

When it has been decided how many representatives the state should have, the state legislature draws up new districts.

What jobs does the House of Representatives have?

Along with the Senate, it considers all important bills. The House has special responsibility for bills that concern money. It passes tax bills to raise money for the government and budget bills to control the government's spending.

How long does a representative serve in the House?

All representatives serve a two-year term, and all of them come up for election at the same time—in November of each even-numbered year. A representative may be reelected over and over again. Some have served in the House for more than forty years.

What are the requirements for a representative?

A representative must have been a citizen of the United States for at least seven years, must be at least twenty-five years old, and must be a resident of the state he or she represents. Until 1917 all representatives were men. In that year, Jeanette Rankin of Montana became the first woman to serve in the House. There have been many others since.

Who runs the meetings of the House?

The Speaker of the House, the most powerful person in the Congress, is nominated by the party that has the most votes in the

House and elected by the whole House. The Speaker runs the meetings of the House and has many other powers.

What Speaker served for the longest time?

Sam Rayburn, a Democrat from Texas, served three different times as Speaker of the House between 1940 and 1961 for a total of nearly seventeen years. He was first elected to the House in 1912 and he was a congressman for more than forty-eight years.

What is the Supreme Court?

The Supreme Court is the highest authority on the laws of the United States. There are nine judges, or justices, on the Court. One of them is the chief justice, and the others are called associate justices.

Are the Supreme Court justices elected?

No. They are appointed by the President and approved by the Senate. Supreme Court justices serve from the day they are sworn into office until their death or resignation.

What does the Supreme Court do?

It hears cases that have been *appealed* from other courts. The court hears arguments from both sides. Then, often months later, it issues a written opinion deciding the case. When the justices cannot agree, they vote on the case. The side supported by the majority of the justices wins.

What are the requirements to sit on the Supreme Court?

The Constitution sets no citizenship or age requirements. All but a few of the justices have been lawyers and active in politics. Many served as judges in lower courts before being appointed to the Supreme Court.

Can a woman be a Supreme Court justice?

Yes. In 1981 Sandra Day O'Connor of Arizona became the first woman justice. She was appointed by President Ronald Reagan.

10

Growing Things, Finding Things, Making Things

What foods were first discovered in America?

Several important foods were never heard of in Europe until the early explorers took them back from America. The most important of all was corn. Indians from many parts of America grew corn as their most important crop. Even today, corn is more important in America than in any other region of the world.

A second group of foods were the squashes, which the Indians grew and ate. These include the pumpkin, which has become a special American treat in pumpkin pies at Thanksgiving.

Then there are white potatoes and sweet potatoes. A funny thing happened to white potatoes. They grew first in Mexico and Central America; then travelers took them back to Europe. The Irish made the potato their favorite starchy food, and when they came to America they brought it with them. So for many years Americans called the white potato the "Irish potato"—even though it came from America in the first place.

What bad habit was first discovered in the Americas?

Using tobacco. The early settlers found that the Indians smoked tobacco in pipes. They took some of the tobacco back to Europe, and soon people there learned to smoke it, too. Tobacco was a very important crop for the early colonists. They sent most of it to Europe and received lots of money for it. Even today the United States produces more tobacco than any other country in the world. The major tobacco states are North Carolina and Tennessee.

If you wanted to be a wheat farmer, what part of the United States would you go to?

Some of the largest wheat farms in the world are on the Great Plains from Texas in the south to North Dakota and Montana in the north. In the southern plains, farmers grow winter wheat, which is planted in the fall, stays alive through the winter, and is harvested the next fall. In the northern plains, farmers grow spring wheat, which is planted in the spring and is ready for harvest in the fall. Some wheat is grown in almost every state of the union.

What is wheat used for?

The most familiar use is in making flour for bread, cakes, and other baked goods. But wheat is also the main ingredient of all pasta products such as spaghetti and macaroni. Wheat can also be used as feed for livestock.

If you wanted to raise corn, what part of the United States would you go to?

The two great corn-producing states are Iowa and Illinois. Other midwestern states also produce large crops.

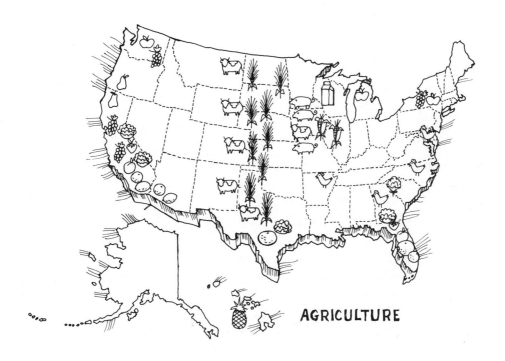

AGRICULTURE

Is this the same corn we eat on the cob or canned or frozen?

No. The grain corn grown in the midwestern states would be very tough to eat. It is almost all used as feed for livestock, especially for cattle and hogs. The corn helps produce our beef and pork. The corn that humans like to eat is *sweet corn,* a special variety that is grown in Wisconsin, Minnesota, and other states.

If you wanted to raise livestock, what state would be best for you?

The most important livestock state in the country is Iowa. The state has more than 25 million cattle and hogs. This means that there are more than eight cattle and hogs for every person in the state. Iowa is the largest hog-raising state in the country. Many of the cattle are raised somewhere else and then shipped to Iowa to be fattened up just before being butchered.

If you wanted to run a cattle ranch, what state would be best for you?

The biggest cattle ranches in the United States are in Texas, which has about 16 million cattle. Other important ranching regions are in the high plains—parts of Oklahoma, New Mexico, Colorado, Kansas, Nebraska, Wyoming, Montana, and the Dakotas.

If you wanted to be a dairy farmer, where might you go?

Wisconsin is known as the dairy state and has more dairy cattle than any other state in the Union. There are dairy farms in many parts of the country, though. Since fresh milk spoils easily, there are usually dairy farming regions within a hundred miles of most large cities.

Where are all the chickens raised?

Chicken is one of the most familiar foods everywhere in the United States. Chickens are grown in almost every state, but the two biggest chicken producers are Arkansas and Georgia. Some other big producers are Alabama, North Carolina, and the Delmarva

Peninsula, which includes parts of Delaware, Maryland, and Virginia. All together, the United States produces and eats over 4 *billion* broiler chickens each year.

Where do fruits come from?

Different fruits come from different parts of the country. Citrus fruits such as oranges, tangerines, grapefruits, and lemons come from only four warm states: Florida, California, Arizona, and Texas. Citrus fruit is the most valuable fruit crop in the United States.

Grapes are good to eat just as they are, and many are also used to make wine, juice, jelly, and raisins. Most grapes come from California, although Washington and New York also have large grape vineyards.

Apples come from states near the northern border. The biggest producer is Washington, followed by New York and Michigan. Many pears come from the states along the Pacific, and peaches come from California, South Carolina, and Georgia, which is sometimes called the Peach State.

Strawberries can be grown almost anywhere, but the biggest producers are California and Florida, where they can be grown all year long. Blueberries grow best in colder climates and sandy soil in such states as Maine, Michigan, and New Jersey.

What is the only state that grows pineapples?

Hawaii. There are huge pineapple plantations in Hawaii that provide millions of the spiny fruits.

Where do vegetables come from?

There are two vegetable-growing regions. One region, where vegetables grow in the summer, takes in most of the country. The other region, where vegetables grow all year long, take in parts of southern California, Arizona, Texas, and Florida. The vegetables we buy during the winter almost always come from this second region. The largest vegetable-producing state is California.

What is the most important farming state in the United States?

The state that grows and sells the most farm products is California. It is also the state that produces the widest variety of farm goods— from milk to wine grapes, and from cotton to oranges. The second most important farming state is Iowa, and Texas is third.

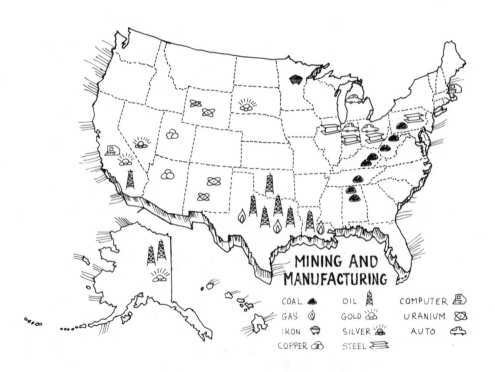

MINING AND MANUFACTURING

COAL 🟤   OIL ⛏   COMPUTER 💻
GAS ◊   GOLD ⛏   URANIUM ⊗
IRON ⬡   SILVER ⛏   AUTO 🚗
COPPER ⬡   STEEL ▤

If you wanted to prospect for gold, where in the United States would you look?

Gold rushes have been very important to the United States. The first large group of Californians were those who came to the state in 1849 looking for gold. Other gold and silver rushes helped bring people to South Dakota, Nevada, and Alaska.

Today most gold and silver are produced by modern mines with sophisticated machinery. But a few prospectors still explore the mountains of the West, hoping to strike it rich. The largest producers of gold are Nevada, South Dakota, and Utah. The most silver comes from Idaho and Arizona. A prospector's best bet would be in one of these states.

Could you prospect for diamonds in the United States?

You could, but you would probably not be very successful. The only state that has any active diamond mines is Arkansas.

Where would you look for uranium?

The states that produce the most uranium are Wyoming and New Mexico. The metal is used to prepare fuel for atomic reactors and weapons. Uranium is radioactive, and its signal can be picked up on a Geiger counter. Most prospectors use these instruments.

Are there other valuable metals in the United States?

Yes. The two most important metals are iron and copper. One of the largest iron ore deposits in the world is near Lake Superior. The iron ore is dug out of huge open-pit mines and placed on barges in the lake. Minnesota produces more than two-thirds of the iron ore in the United States each year.

Copper ore occurs in the western states. The largest producer is Arizona. One of the largest single mines in the world is in Utah.

Where does oil come from?

Oil comes from wells that pump the dark, thick liquid up from deep under the ground. Oil is the product of plants that lived millions of years ago and have been underground under tremendous pressure and heat for centuries. We use oil as a fuel to heat buildings and run generators that produce electricity; as the main source of gasoline and diesel fuel to run cars, trucks, and locomotives; as an important ingredient in plastics; and as a lubricant in machinery.

Is there oil in the United States?

Yes. There is not enough to meet our needs, so we also buy oil from other countries. But we produce more than 3 billion barrels of oil a year in the United States.

What states does the oil come from?

Oil comes from three major regions. The largest is in the southern states of Texas, Louisiana, and Oklahoma. The newest source of oil is in the northern part of Alaska. In the 1970s a huge pipeline was built from the oil wells near the Arctic Ocean across the middle of Alaska to Valdez, a port town on the Pacific Ocean. The pipeline can carry several million barrels a day over more than 1,000 miles. The third oil region is in southern California. Together, these three regions produce most of the oil in the United States.

What is natural gas?

Natural gas is a colorless, odorless gas that can be burned as a fuel for heating or for cooking. Like oil, it is pumped from under the ground, and it often occurs in the same region where oil has been found.

If natural gas is odorless, why does the gas used in stoves have a smell?

Gas companies add the familiar smell to the gas to make it safer to use. Since we can smell it, we know when some gas is leaking. If the gas had no smell, we would not notice a leak, and a gas leak could cause an explosion.

Is there natural gas in the United States?

Yes. The two states that produce the largest amount are Texas and Louisiana.

Is the natural gas shipped by tanker truck?

No. Most of it is transported through underground pipelines. A network of natural gas lines covers most of the United States. The gas used in a kitchen stove in New England may travel 1,500 miles by pipeline from Louisiana.

Are there other important fuels?

Yes. The most important other fuel is coal. People once used coal to heat their homes. Today it is used mostly to power generators that make electricity and in the manufacture of steel.

Is there coal in the United States?

Yes. Some of the largest deposits of coal in the world are in the United States. The most productive areas are in the Appalachian Mountains from Alabama north into Pennsylvania. The largest coal-producing states are Kentucky and West Virginia. In recent years, new mining techniques have increased the production of coal in Wyoming, which is now third.

What is steel?

Steel is iron that has been separated from the iron ore, purified, and mixed with small amounts of other metals to provide the right combination of qualities. Steel is used to make automobiles, refrigerators, huge beams that become the framework of new buildings, and many other products.

How is steel made?

Making steel requires about five main ingredients: iron, coal, limestone, and huge amounts of air and water. The iron is melted and "cooked" at high temperatures with coke (which is made from the coal), limestone, and air. This cooking process makes the impurities in the iron come to the top, where they can be gotten rid of. Then small amounts of other metals are mixed with the iron, and the liquid metal is ready to be cooled. The water is used for cooling.

Where is steel made in the United States?

Most of the steel is made in a narrow belt of land between Chicago and Pittsburgh, Pennsylvania. Major steel centers are Pittsburgh; Youngstown and Cleveland, Ohio; and Gary, Indiana.

This steel-making area may receive its iron ore from barges on the Great Lakes, coal from the coal regions of West Virginia and Kentucky, limestone from quarries in the Midwest, and water from the Great Lakes or from a major river.

Steel companies in other parts of the world have found new methods to make steel less expensively, so much steel used today in the United States is imported from other countries.

Where are cars made in the United States?

The capital of the automobile business is Detroit, Michigan. The four largest manufacturers have their main offices in or near Detroit, and many large auto assembly plants are located there. Factories in surrounding areas of Michigan, Indiana, and Ohio produce important parts for the cars—tires, batteries, stamped metal pieces for the auto bodies, and engine parts.

There are also assembly plants in other parts of the country, however. Many familiar American makes of cars are assembled in southern California, in the South, or in the Northeast.

Are computers made in any particular place?

No, computers are not assembled in a particular region of the country, but there are two places where the work of developing new computers is centered. One area is just south of San Francisco, California. It is sometimes called Silicon Valley, because the microchips that are the heart of the computers are made of silicon, the main ingredient of sand. Another similar cluster of computer companies is just outside Boston, Massachusetts.

What is the largest construction project in world history?

Many people say it is the United States Interstate Highway System. The system was planned in the 1950s and is being completed in the 1980s. When finished it will have 43,000 miles of multi-lane road. The interstate system has roads in every state except Alaska and connects nearly all cities with 100,000 population or more. Most of the money for the Interstate System came from taxes on gasoline.

Why do we need dams?

A dam can do many useful things. It can control a river that floods often and causes great suffering and destruction. It can store up water for people to use to water crops in desert places or to use in homes and factories. And it can help make electrical power.

What is the largest dam in the United States?

Dams are measured in different ways, and no two ways give the same winner. The highest one in the United States is the Oroville Dam across the Feather River in northern California. It is 756 feet high—the height of a 60-story skyscraper—and its rim is 1¼ miles long. The Oroville Dam is made of earth-fill—some 78 million cubic yards of earth, sand, gravel, and rock.

The second highest is Hoover Dam on the Colorado River in Nevada. It is 726 feet high, almost as high as the Oroville Dam. But it is only about a quarter of a mile wide. The dam plugs a narrow canyon and is made of concrete. It created a huge man-made lake, Lake Mead, which stretches some 115 miles behind the dam. An *aqueduct* or water tunnel carries water from the dam 240 miles to southern California. Generators at the dam make electric power that is sent by high tension wires to cities in California and Arizona. In addition, the dam provides enough water each year to irrigate a million acres of land.

The largest dam in the world in volume was completed in 1973 in Arizona. It is called the New Cornelia Tailings, and it has 274 million cubic yards of material—enough to fill more than 90 million dump trucks.

Why do we need tunnels?

The earliest of modern tunnels were built to carry water long distances. Very deep water tunnels connect major cities to streams and lakes in the countryside, sometimes more than 100 miles away.

Builders of railroads in the 1800s needed tunnels to avoid sending trains up and down very steep mountains. Later, similar tunnels were built to allow cars and other vehicles to drive through high mountains.

A third reason for building tunnels is to allow trains or cars to cross a river or other body of water. Sometimes a tunnel is easier and less expensive to build than a bridge.

Where are the longest land tunnels?

The longest tunnels by far are those for railroads in Japan and Europe. The Seikan railroad tunnel in Japan, which is just being completed, will be the longest—33½ miles. The Simplon Tunnels between Switzerland and Italy, which are more than sixty years old, burrow under huge mountains for more than 12 miles. The longest in the United States is the Cascade railroad tunnel in the state of Washington, which is nearly 8 miles long.

Where are the longest land tunnels for cars and other vehicles?

The longest are in Europe. The St. Gotthard tunnel, in Switzerland, which opened in 1980, is more than 10 miles long. There are many shorter tunnels in the United States. The Dwight D. Eisenhower Memorial Tunnel carries traffic on Interstate 70 more than 1⅕ miles under a huge mountain in Colorado. A long series of highway tunnels burrow through the Appalachian Mountains on the Pennsylvania Turnpike.

Where are the longest underwater tunnels?

The longest underwater tunnel in the United States is the Trans-Bay Tubes built under San Francisco Bay for use by subway trains.

The tubes are more than 3½ miles long. The longest underwater road tunnels enter the island of Manhattan in New York City. They are:

Tunnel	Water-crossing	Length
Brooklyn-Battery	East River	9,117 feet (1¾ mi.)
Holland Tunnel	Hudson River	8,557 feet (1⅝ mi.)
Lincoln Tunnel	Hudson River	8,216 feet (1½ mi.)

There are other long tunnels under Chesapeake Bay in Maryland and Virginia.

How is the length of a bridge measured?

A bridge is usually measured from one *pier* to the other. A pier is one of the foundations the bridge rests on. The distance between the piers is called the *span* of the bridge. Bridges are not usually measured for their total length from where they leave land to where they return to land.

What kind of bridge has the longest span?

The suspension bridge can stretch nearly a mile (5,280 feet) from one pier, or support, to the next and so has the longest span. Other kinds of bridges are good for distances of less than 2,000 feet.

What was the first great suspension bridge?

The most famous early suspension bridge is the Brooklyn Bridge, which connects Manhattan and Brooklyn, across the East River. It opened in May 1883 and had a span of 1,600 feet. In May 1983, the Brooklyn Bridge observed its 100th birthday with a huge celebration. The Brooklyn Bridge is not the longest suspension bridge anymore, but it is still in service and is still one of the most beautiful bridges in America.

What are the longest suspension bridges in the United States?

Four bridges span 3,500 feet or more:

Bridge	Location	Water crossing	Span length
Verrazano-Narrows	New York	New York Bay	4,260 feet
Golden Gate	San Francisco	San Francisco Bay	4,200 feet
Mackinac	Northern Michigan	Straits of Mackinac	3,800 feet
George Washington	New York	Hudson River	3,500 feet

What is the longest water-crossing by road in the United States?

The longest crossing is probably the Chesapeake Bay Bridge-Tunnel. It stretches 17.6 miles between mainland Virginia and the Eastern Shore of the Delmarva Peninsula. It consists of twelve miles of trestles (road built on stilts over shallow water), four man-made islands, two bridges, and two underwater tunnels, each a mile long.

What is the tallest building in the United States?

The Sears Tower in Chicago is the tallest. It has 110 stories and measures 1,454 feet from the ground to the roof. A television antenna on the roof adds another 350 feet for a total of 1,804 feet.

There are six buildings in the United States that stand over 1,000 feet from the ground to the roof. They are:

Building, City	Height
Sears Tower, Chicago	1,454 feet
World Trade Center (2 towers), New York	1,350 feet
Empire State Building, New York	1,250 feet
Standard Oil Building, Chicago	1,136 feet
John Hancock Building, Chicago	1,127 feet
Chrysler Building, New York	1,046 feet

Are these the tallest man-made buildings in the world?

No. The CN Tower in Toronto, Canada, stands 1,821 feet high. It is not an office building, but an observation tower. It is the tallest self-supporting structure in the world.

Some television antennas in South Dakota and in the Soviet Union are more than 2,000 feet high, but they are fastened to the ground with guy wires, so are not self-supporting.

11

Things to See and Do

Where is Niagara Falls?

Niagara Falls is in the Niagara River, which connects two of the Great Lakes—Erie and Ontario. The river forms part of the border between Canada and the United States; one part of the falls is in Canada, and the other part is in the United States.

Is Niagara Falls the highest falls in the United States?

No, not at all. The water at Niagara Falls drops about 167 feet. One waterfall in the United States is almost *ten times* that high.

Then why is Niagara so famous?

Most waterfalls are narrow ribbons of water. Together, Niagara's two main falls are more than two-thirds of a mile wide, and every minute 200,000 tons of water pour over them. The roar of the falls is so loud that people standing nearby must shout to each other to be heard. And the spray can sometimes soak people standing half a mile away.

The larger of the two falls, called the Horseshoe Falls, is in Canada. The American Falls is in the United States. The sister cities of Niagara Falls, Ontario, and Niagara Falls, New York, stand on either side. Visitors can cross the river by bridge to see the falls from both sides.

Does water ever stop falling at Niagara?

Yes. If a winter is very cold, the Niagara River and the falls can freeze. Also, in 1969 American engineers stopped the American Falls by building a temporary dam upstream so that they could study the rock at the edge of the falls.

Has Niagara Falls always looked the same?

No. The rushing water gradually erodes, or eats away, the rock at the edge of the falls. Since the 1600s the Horseshoe Falls has moved upstream nearly a quarter of a mile. The American Falls has moved upstream about 90 feet in the same period. Scientists believe that thousands of years ago, both falls were many miles downstream.

What is the highest waterfall in the United States?

The Ribbon Falls in Yosemite (yo-SEM-i-tee) National Park drops more than 1,600 feet into the Merced River. During part of the year—from late summer into the spring—the Ribbon Falls may be dry.

There are several other beautiful waterfalls in the Yosemite Valley. Upper Yosemite Falls is more than 1,430 feet high.

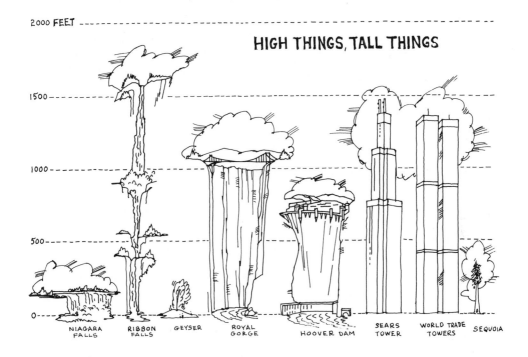

HIGH THINGS, TALL THINGS

2000 FEET

1500

1000

500

0

NIAGARA FALLS   RIBBON FALLS   GEYSER   ROYAL GORGE   HOOVER DAM   SEARS TOWER   WORLD TRADE TOWERS   SEQUOIA

Are there high falls in other parts of the world?

Only a few. The highest waterfall of all is Angel Falls in Venezuela. Its main fall is a drop of 2,650 feet—a little more than half a mile, and nearly twice the height of the world's tallest skyscraper.

Where are the largest caves in the United States?

No one knows for sure where the largest caves are, since there are many that are still unexplored. The longest system of caves known in the world is the Mammoth Cave system in central Kentucky. The caves are in Mammoth Cave National Park.

The Mammoth Caves are like a dark underground country. More than 170 miles of caves are known, and they include several underground rivers and lakes. Parts of the cave system are lighted so that visitors can see the fantastic rock formations in beautiful colors. Nearly two million visitors come to see them each year.

A second national park preserves the Carlsbad Caverns in New Mexico. These caverns run much deeper than the Mammoth Caves. Visitors can take an elevator more than 800 feet (about 70 stories!) down from the entrance level. One great chamber in the caverns is three quarters of a mile long and more than 600 feet wide.

What is a geyser?

A geyser is a special kind of hot water spring. Instead of bubbling gently out of the ground, the hot water of a geyser shoots out with great force. Some geysers shoot water and steam as high as 400 feet in the air. They are usually quiet for hours or days; then they suddenly erupt for a few minutes.

The water in narrow crevices deep underground heats up to very high temperatures. This superheated water cannot escape at first because there is a huge column of cooler water above it. Finally, when enough water is superheated, it turns to steam. As the steam expands, it heats the upper layer of water and pushes it toward the surface of the earth with tremendous force. After water and steam have been shot out into the air, the narrow crevices fill again with cooler water. When this new supply is superheated, the geyser erupts again.

Where can you see geysers?

Only one place in the United States has a large number of geysers: Yellowstone National Park, in the northwest corner of Wyoming. The most famous of all the geysers is Old Faithful. It gets its name because it erupts on a fairly regular schedule—every 65 minutes on the average. Many other geysers and hot springs are scattered across the huge park. In addition, there are beautiful mountains and lakes, many wild animals, and miles of hiking trails. More than two million visitors come to see Yellowstone Park each year.

What is a canyon?

A canyon is a kind of valley, usually one with steep rock sides. Canyons are almost always made by rivers. Over many thousands of years, the river cuts away at the rock, forming a deep valley for itself. Once the canyon walls start to form, wind and rain help to wear them away.

What is the biggest canyon in the United States?

The biggest canyon in the United States, and in the world, is the Grand Canyon. The Grand Canyon is part of the Colorado River basin in northern Arizona. The canyon runs for some 200 miles, and there is a drop from the rim to the bottom of as much as a mile (5,280 feet). The distance between the two rims ranges from 4 miles to more than 10 miles.

The walls of the Grand Canyon show many different layers of rock. They are of different colors and different hardnesses, and have been worn away at different speeds. Earth scientists have learned much about the earth's history by comparing recent layers of rock near the top to very old layers of rock near the bottom of the canyon.

Is the Grand Canyon the deepest canyon in the United States?

No. Hells Canyon is the deepest canyon. It is on the Snake River on the Idaho-Oregon state line, about 100 miles south of Lewiston, Idaho. The average height of the canyon is about a mile above the river, and at some places the river is almost 8,000 feet below the rim. Hells Canyon is not nearly as long or as wide as the Grand Canyon, but it is deeper.

What bridge is highest above the river it crosses?

The Royal Gorge Suspension Bridge in Colorado. Royal Gorge, a narrow canyon on the Arkansas River, is more than 1,000 feet deep. The suspension bridge that crosses the gorge is 1,056 feet above the level of the river.

What is the longest hiking trail in the United States?

The Appalachian Trail follows the line of the Appalachian Mountains for almost 2,000 miles from Maine to Georgia. It runs through fourteen states, and is one of the most popular hiking trails in the world. Some hikers have spent many years hiking one part of the trail at a time until they have seen it all. But most people only hike a small part of the trail, often one near their home. The Appalachian Trail became a part of the U.S. National Park System in 1968.

Are there other long hiking trails?

Yes. There is a Pacific Crest system of trails along the Cascade and Sierra Nevada Mountains through Washington, Oregon, and California. But this trail system is not continuous like the Appalachian Trail.

What is a National Park?

A National Park is land that is set aside because of its scenic beauty. National Parks are cared for by the U.S. National Park Service. The first—and still the largest—National Park is Yellowstone. It was set aside in 1872 and contains almost 3,500 square miles. Other famous National Parks include the Grand Canyon in Arizona, Yosemite in California, the Everglades in Florida, Mammoth Cave in Kentucky, and many others.

Are there other National Park lands?

Yes. There are National Recreation Areas and National Lakeshores and Seashores, which preserve places for swimming, hiking, fishing, camping, and other recreation. The two largest are along the shores of Lake Mead and Lake Powell, the huge manmade lakes behind giant dams in Arizona, Nevada, and Utah. There are also more than eighty National Monuments. These preserve other places of natural beauty or historical importance.

The National Park System also includes many Historic Sites, National Memorials, Military Parks, and battlefields. These include the birthplaces of many famous Americans, important monuments to national heroes, and the major battlefields of the American Revolution and the Civil War.

Where is the Statue of Liberty and where did it come from?

The Statue of Liberty is a huge copper-covered statue that stands on Liberty Island, a small island in New York harbor. It rises 151 feet high on a pedestal 154 feet high. Liberty is shown as a proud woman in flowing robes. In her right hand she holds a torch and in her left a tablet that bears the date of the signing Declaration of Independence.

The statue was a gift of the people of France to the people of the United States. Frederic Bartholdi, a French sculptor, designed the statue, and a representative of the French people made the gift in 1884. The statue was shipped to America in pieces in 1885 and

THINGS TO SEE

was assembled on its pedestal in 1886. It was dedicated by President Grover Cleveland on October 28, 1886. It is a National Monument and is usually open to visitors, who arrive on a sightseeing boat from the foot of Manhattan Island in New York City.

Where is Ellis Island?

Ellis Island is another small island in the harbor of New York City near the Statue of Liberty. From 1891 to 1954, Ellis Island was the first place most immigrants to the United States landed. While on the island, their immigration papers were checked, and they received a physical examination to see that they had no dangerous diseases. In its sixty-three years as an immigration center, more than sixteen million immigrants passed through.

What do Mount Vernon, Monticello, and Hyde Park have in common?

Each was the home of a President. Mount Vernon, in northern Virginia, was the home of George Washington. Monticello was the home designed by Thomas Jefferson near Charlottesville, Virginia. He retired to Monticello after serving as President. Hyde Park, north of New York City on the Hudson River, was the estate of Franklin Delano Roosevelt. These Presidents' homes and others are cared for by the National Park Service and are open to visitors.

In what city can you visit monuments to Washington and Lincoln?

In Washington, D.C. The Washington Monument is a tall, pointed structure called an obelisk, standing 555 feet high. The Lincoln Memorial is a large marble building containing a huge statue of Lincoln.

There are many other important monuments and buildings in Washington. From the grounds of the Washington Monument, a visitor can see the White House, where the President lives and works; the Capitol, where Congress meets; and the Jefferson and Lincoln Memorials. There is a National Visitors' Center in Washington, where the National Park Service gives directions to all the sights of the capital city.

What is the largest monument to American Presidents?

Mount Rushmore in the Black Hills of South Dakota. There the sculptor Gutzon Borglum spent fourteen years carving the faces of four great Presidents: Washington, Jefferson, Theodore Roosevelt, and Abraham Lincoln. Borglum died before the huge job was finished, and the face of Lincoln was completed by his son. The face of Washington is 60 feet high, and those of the other Presidents are in proportion. Mount Rushmore is a National Monument.

What are the famous museums in America?

There are too many even to list here. First a visitor must decide what kind of museum to look for. Some museums show famous works of art. Others have exhibits about plants and animals. Others have exhibits about science and inventions. Still others have exhibits about history.

What is the most famous art museum in America?

The Metropolitan Museum of Art in New York City is the largest and probably the most famous. It has many paintings and statues by famous artists of all countries and times. Another famous art museum is the Museum of Modern Art, also in New York. Most of its paintings and sculptures have been done in the last one hundred years. Chicago, Boston, Los Angeles, Dallas, Washington, and other large cities have other important art museums.

What museums have exhibits about plants and animals?

These museums are often called "natural history" museums. Two of the largest are the Field Museum of Natural History in Chicago and the Museum of Natural History in New York.

What museums have exhibits about science and technology?

The Museum of Science and Industry in Chicago is one of the largest in the world. It has many exhibits that visitors can operate. The National Air and Space Museum is a part of the Smithsonian Institution in Washington, D.C. It has the Wright Brothers' first airplane and many other famous planes, rockets, and space capsules.

Where else are there exhibits on space?

There are two centers of American space flight. One is the John F. Kennedy Space Center on Cape Canaveral near Cocoa Beach, Florida. From here, manned and unmanned spacecraft are launched into space with huge rockets. When a launching is scheduled, thousands of people gather to see it.

The second important place for space flight is the Lyndon B. Johnson Space Center in Houston, Texas. It is the "nerve center" for all American manned space flights. Astronauts train there, new rockets are designed there, and when a flight is underway, it is tracked by the people and computers at the Houston center.

What museums have exhibits about history?

There are many museums about history. Some are in famous old houses where a famous person lived or worked. Others are in a place where something important happened. At Gettysburg, Pennsylvania, there are museums which show the weapons and uniforms soldiers used during the Battle of Gettysburg during the Civil War.

One of the most famous historical places is Williamsburg, Virginia, which is both a town and a kind of museum. In the 1700s, Williamsburg was the capital of the colony of Virginia. In the 1900s, part of the town was *restored* to look just as it looked in the 1700s. More than a million people visit Williamsburg each year.

Are there special museums for particular subjects?

Yes. A famous special museum is the Baseball Hall of Fame in the small town of Cooperstown, New York. The Hall of Fame Museum honors the greatest baseball players of the past. It shows their uniforms, gloves, bats, and other equipment. There are also plaques for each player who has been voted into the Hall of Fame.

Another sports museum is the Professional Football Hall of Fame in Canton, Ohio.

Other special museums are for early automobiles, railroad equipment and history, and many other special subjects.

Where are the greatest zoos in America?

Zoos are different from museums because they show living things. The largest zoo in America is the San Diego Zoo in California, which shows more than 1,600 kinds of animals. The San Diego Zoological Society also operates a Wild Animal Park outside the city where animals can be seen in the open.

Other large zoos include the Bronx Zoo in New York City, the National Zoological Park in Washington, D.C., and others in St. Louis, Chicago, and Milwaukee.

Are there any specialized zoos?

Yes. One of the most famous is the Arizona-Sonora Desert Zoo in Tucson, Arizona. It shows desert animals. Another kind of specialized zoo shows water creatures. Marineland of the Pacific in Long Beach, California, and two Sea Worlds in San Diego, California, and Orlando, Florida, are examples. They exhibit hundreds of kinds of fish including giant sharks, and many sea mammals including whales.

What are the most popular amusement parks in the United States?

Disneyland in Anaheim, California, and Disneyworld near Orlando, Florida, attract tens of millions of visitors every year. They offer rides, shows, and other amusements for children and adults. Many of the attractions feature characters from famous Walt Disney movies and television productions. In 1982, a new park called Epcot was opened near Disneyworld in Florida. It has many exhibits about new inventions and technology.

Where would you go to learn about the movies?

The home of the movie industry is Hollywood, California. Hollywood is not really a city, but a part of the city of Los Angeles. Large movie studios were built in Hollywood beginning in the 1920s. Today many of the movies made there are for television.

What is there to see in Hollywood?

There are several famous movie theaters along Hollywood Boulevard. In front of one of them, many famous movie stars have made their handprints or footprints in the concrete. Some nearby movie studios offer tours. And many visitors enjoy seeing the nearby town of Beverly Hills, where many well-known movie stars have homes.

Where would you go to learn about television?

Almost every city has a local television station, and a visit to one of these can teach a lot about TV. The large television networks have major offices and studios in New York City and somewhere in or near Hollywood. Some of the studios offer tours, and some shows are broadcast or recorded with live audiences. If you want tickets to a show, you should write or call the network that broadcasts it.

Where would you go to learn about recorded music?

New York and Hollywood are also recording centers where many of the most popular records are made. Another recording capital is

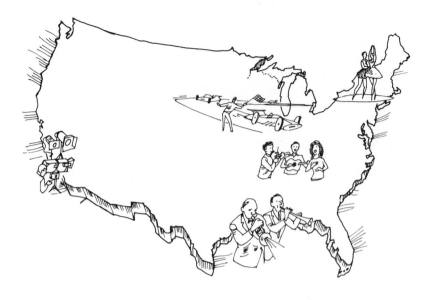

ENTERTAINMENT

Nashville, Tennessee. Many popular Country and Western recordings are made in Nashville. The city is also the home of the Grand Ole Opry, a famous radio and television show featuring Country and Western music.

If you wanted to learn about the theater, where would you go?

The center of the theater in America is New York City. For many years, the most famous plays and musicals have been presented in theaters on or near the major street called Broadway. So a popular play or musical is often called a Broadway show. There are also many smaller theaters in other parts of New York, and they are called Off-Broadway theaters. Off-Broadway theaters present many new plays by young writers and use young actors and actresses.

There are many well-known theaters in other cities. These theaters present both new plays and classic plays from the past. In smaller cities and towns, local colleges and universities often present plays.

If you wanted to learn about opera or ballet, where would you go?

Several large cities now have ballet and opera companies. But New York City is also the most important center for these arts.

What is the most famous auto race in America?

The Indianapolis 500 is a race run on Memorial Day weekend in late May each year. It is run at the Indianapolis International Speedway in Indiana. Each year it attracts about 500,000 spectators. Other famous races are run each year at Daytona Beach, Florida, and at "super-tracks" in Atlanta; Talladega, Alabama; and Darlington, South Carolina.

Where is the most famous horse race in America?

The most famous race each year is the Kentucky Derby, which is run at the Churchill Downs race track in Louisville, Kentucky. It attracts more than 200,000 people and is watched by millions more on television.

What is the largest crowd attracted each year in America?

The largest crowd is the one that watches the Parade of Roses each New Year's Day in Pasadena, California. The parade includes large floats decorated with thousands of flowers, marching bands, horse teams, and guest celebrities. About two million people line the 8-mile-long parade route each year.

The Rose Bowl football game, played on New Year's afternoon, is between two champion college teams. It was the first of many bowl games that are now played on New Year's. In the 1984 Olympics, the Rose Bowl Stadium was used for the soccer competition.

Index

Rankin, Jeannette, 145
Rayburn, Sam, 146
Reagan, Ronald, 133, 136, 147
redwood (tree), 66
Revere, Paul, 114
Revolutionary War, 85, 86, 113, 114–118
Rhode Island, 21
Rhode Island Red (bird), 72
Ribbon Falls, 170
Rio Grande (river), 12, 43
Roanoke Island, 81
Roanoke River, 44
Rochester, New York, 57
Rocky Mountains, 37–38, 39
Roosevelt, Alice, 138
Roosevelt, Eleanor, 140–141
Roosevelt, Franklin D., 134, 138
Roosevelt, Theodore, 136, 138, 140, 177
rose, 68
Rose Bowl (football game), 184
Royal Gorge, Colorado, 174
Rushmore, Mount, South Dakota, 177
Russia, 85
    see also Soviet Union

S

Sacajawea, 87–88
Samoset, 83
St. Augustine, Florida, 81
St. Helens, Mount, Washington, 46
St. Lawrence River, 41, 43
St. Lawrence Seaway, 41, 42
St. Louis, Missouri, 15, 43
San Andreas Fault, 48
San Antonio, Texas, 34, 121
San Diego, California, 55
San Francisco, California, 55
San Jacinto, Battle of, 121
San-San, 34
Santa Ana (wind), 61
Santa Anna (Mexican general), 121
Santa Fe Trail, 102
Saratoga, Battle of, 116
Savannah River, 44
Scandinavia, settlers from, 105–106
sea gull (bird), 69
Sears Tower, Chicago, 165, 166
sequoia (tree), 65, 66

Sequoia National Park, 65
Seward, William H., 88
Sherman, William Tecumseh, 127
Siberia, 79
Silver Lake, Colorado, 56
Sioux Indians, 128–129
skyscrapers, 165–166
    table of highest, 166
slavery, 121–122
Smith, Margaret Chase, 144
snow, 56–57
Snowbelt, The, 32
South (region), 29–30
South Cape, Hawaii, 14
South Dakota, 90
South Pass, 99
Soviet Union, 10, 11, 13
    see also Russia
Spain, 85, 88, 96
Squanto, 83
squashes, 151
Standard Oil Building, Chicago, 166
starling (bird), 73
Star Spangled Banner, 119
states, 19–31
    admission to United States, 89–91
    area of, 20–23; table, 22
    birds, 70–72; table, 71
    capitals, 26–28; table, 27–28
    flowers, 68–70; table, 70
    ocean shoreline, 25
    population density, 24
    population table, 23
    trees, 67–68; table, 67
Statue of Liberty, 175–176
steel, 160
storms, 58–62
Sumter, Fort, South Carolina, 123
Sunbelt, The, 32
sunflower, 68
sunny places, 57
Superior, Lake, 41
Susquehanna River, 44

T

Taft, William Howard, 139
Tamarack, California, 56
television, 181

Wisconsin, 74
wolf, 76
wolverine, 74–75
World Trade Center, New York City, 166
World War II, 113, 130
Wounded Knee, South Dakota, 129–130
Wrangell, Mount, Alaska, 47
Wright Brothers, 178
Wyoming, 21, 61

Y

Yellowstone National Park, 172–173, 175
Yorktown, Siege of, 116
Yosemite Falls, 170
Yuma, Arizona, 57

Z

zoos, 180